Anniversaries to Celebrate

Anniversaries to Celebrate

BY

Verle C. Schumacher

The Pilgrim Press   *New York*

Library of Congress Cataloging in Publication Data

Schumacher, Verle, C., 1924–
  Anniversaries to celebrate.

  Bibliography
  1. United Church of Christ—History. I. Title.
BX9884.S38   1983   285.8'34   83–2228
ISBN 0-8298-0628-8

The Pilgrim Press, 132 West 31 Street, New York, N.Y. 10001

CONTENTS

Contents

Contents

vii

Contents

Contents

Contents

x

INTRODUCTION

List all the desired results of the denomination-wide recognition in 1982 of the twenty-fifth anniversary of the founding of the United Church of Christ, and I will add another that might not appear upon your list: This observance may well be the most consciousness-raising event with regard to church-sponsored anniversaries that has occurred so far in the life of this denomination. It probably has wakened many members of the United Church of Christ—both clergy and lay—to the educational and faith-deepening values of such celebrations, and it may prompt church leaders and congregations to plan the observance of other significant church anniversaries in the future.

Not that the denomination has been unaware of the importance of recognizing anniversaries. In 1975 the Pennsylvania Southeast Conference observed with historical drama and special services the 250th anniversary of the first communion service of the German Reformed Church in the United States. October 1981 was designated Haystack Recognition Month for congregations of the United Church of Christ, celebrating the 175th anniversary of that day in 1806 when five Williams College students took shelter from rain behind a haystack and, while huddled there, decided to dedicate their lives to Christ's mission overseas. Though the awareness already exists, one can hope that the 1982 recognition of the denomination's twenty-fifth birthday has stimulated congregations to do much more in taking advantage of the values that accompany significant church anniversary observances.

Lutherans have planned to celebrate the 500th anniversary of the birth of Martin Luther in 1983 in a great festival to be held at Erfurt. But Luther does not belong only to Lutherans. Members of the United Church of Christ should regard Luther's life and work as a significant part of their heritage.

One of the four historical streams that formed the United Church of Christ, the Evangelical Synod of North America traces its beginnings back to Luther. In the early 1800s the distinctions between the Lutheran and Reformed movements in Germany had become outdated as far as many were concerned, though a lively rivalry still prevailed. In 1817, marking the 300th anniversary of the beginning of the Protestant Reformation, Frederick William III, king of Prussia, insisted by law that the Evangelical Lutherans and the Evangelical Reformed stop quarreling over petty differences and become one Evangelical Church.

Many of the German Evangelicals later emigrated to the United States and Canada, forming what eventually became known as the Evangelical Synod of North America. Confirmation instruction in congregations belonging to the Synod was based on Luther's Small Catechism and the Heidelberg Catechism. Furthermore, the Augsburg Confession, Luther's Catechism and the Heidelberg Catechism were regarded as the Synod's theological guides.

In 1980 the German Democratic Republic synod of the

Introduction

Evangelische Kirche der Union (EKU) voted unanimously to enter into *Kirchengemeinschaft,* or "full communion", with the United Church of Christ. Within a month the other synod of the EKU—in the Federal Republic of Germany—affirmed the same resolution. At the General Synod at Rochester, N.Y., June, 1981, a delegation of three pastors and one lay leader from the two synods of the Evangelical Church in Germany was present to symbolize the German proffer of *Kirchengemeinschaft.* It was a high moment of the General Synod when the delegates voted to acknowledge the special bond between the United Church of Christ and the *Evangelische Kirche der Union* (EKU). As successor of the Evangelical Church of Prussia, the Evangelical Church in Germany is both Lutheran and Reformed in its historical heritage, tracing its beginnings directly back to Martin Luther.

In this context, I have been prompted to lift up possible significant church anniversaries that United Church of Christ congregations could meaningfully observe in 1983 and beyond. Included are anniversaries of events connected with the founding and migrations of the four denominations that became the United Church of Christ, deaths of great leaders of those denominations, publication dates of hymns and significant writings by persons of the Congregational-Christian and Evangelical and Reformed traditions, and of a variety of other events in the denomination's history.

These suggestions for church anniversary observances in United Church of Christ congregations are presented with the hope that they will stimulate historical research into the denomination's four-fold tradition and will stimulate creative planning of other anniversary celebrations in years to come.

There is a good theological reason why we Christians should observe anniversaries. The God of Christians

xiii

and Jews is not a nature god who is revealed in the vegetative processes of death and renewal in nature's seasonal cycles. Ours is a God whose self-revelation is through mighty acts in history. God acts in persons and events in linear time to fulfill His loving and redeeming purposes. This is the God who called Abraham out of Ur in Babylon, with the promise to make him the father of a great people. This is the God who delivered the children of Israel out of bondage in Egypt; an event that Jews celebrate regularly in their *Seder* meal. This is the God who entered into a covenant relationship with Israel at Sinai, calling them to be a special people with special responsibilities. This is the God who led the Israelites to the Promised Land, who spoke through the prophets, who led this people in their return from the Exile, and who, in the fullness of time, was revealed in the life, death and resurrection of Our Saviour, Jesus Christ. As the Apostle Paul put it, "God was in Christ, reconciling the world to Himself" (2 Corinthians 5:19), and as the writer of the Fourth Gospel stated it, "The Word became flesh and dwelt among us (John 1:14)." This God, through the Holy Spirit, has been active in the life of the church century after century; always working in mysterious and marvelous ways.

By celebrating the anniversaries of significant persons and events in the Church's history we are celebrating "God at work"; recognizing that the God who has acted in and through persons and events in the past, continues to act in and through persons and events in the life of people today. God's people are a people with a memory, and that is important. Remembering God's actions in past centuries enables us to be receptive to God's Spirit today and enables us to be open to allow God to fulfill the divine purposes through us as channels of God's love and instruments of God's peace.

Anniversaries of the Evangelical Stream

The 500th Anniversary of The Birth of Martin Luther (1483)[1]

Martin Luther was born on November 10, in a modest cottage in Eisleben, Thuringia. As was the custom at the time, his parents took the child to the parish church the next day to be baptized. There they named him Martin, after the saint whose martyrdom was commemorated on November 11th. Six other children were to follow.

Hans Luther, his father, was stern and rugged, with a tendency to become angry. He was also short, heavy-set, and ambitious. He was descended from a long line of Saxon peasant farmers and had labored as a farmer at Mohra. Six months after Martin was born, Hans Luther took his family to Mansfeld where he went into copper-mining, hoping to better his lot in life and that of his family.

Margaret, his mother, was timid, modest, and much given to prayer. Both parents were frugal and industrious. Luther, later recalling his childhood wrote: "My father, as a young man, was a poor miner. My mother gathered firewood in the forest and carried home on her back all that was needed in the house. The harsh conditions forced them to work hard." As the result of such hard work and thrift the family's fortune began to rise.

At Mansfeld, Hans Luther gained respect and was

3

elevated in social status. Eventually he was prosperous enough to lease and manage several copper mines and could begin to dream of greater things for his oldest son. For his class, two dignified professions were within reach of the boy; law and the church. Though he was a religious man, Hans Luther despised priests and opposed his son's becoming one. Like many in his class, Hans did not regard the monastic life as very desirable. How could any priest take care of his parents in their old age and how could he pass on the ancestral name if he had no family? He hoped that, someday, Martin would make a name for himself as a lawyer. Perhaps Martin would gain a position in the court of Duke Frederick and might marry a young woman from a reputable family. Martin later wrote to his father: "You planned for me a respectable and wealthy marriage."

Hans and Margaret Luther were determined that their son would be trained in character, hard work and piety; they knew that such training began in the home. As was common in the Middle Ages, they took quite seriously the proverb: "He who spares the rod hates his son, but he who loves him is diligent to discipline him" (Proverbs 13:24). Recalling his childhood, Luther later wrote: "My father once whipped me so that I ran away from him and felt ugly toward him until he took pains to win me back." He also wrote, "Once my mother whipped me till the blood came, for taking a nut. Such strict discipline drove me to the monastery, though she meant well." He noted that circumstances were not always taken into account and that the severity of punishment was most unfair.

Martin Luther was never really estranged from his parents, however. Though the general atmosphere of his home was probably more somber than joyful, there was much evidence of good cheer, caring, love, and concern. The isolated remark connecting family discipline with the vow to enter the monastery was probably overemphasized. It is quite apparent that, later in life Luther showed a great deal of affection and deep respect for his parents. When Hans Luther suffered from his final illness, Martin wanted his parents to come and live with him in Wittenberg. He wrote, "I would be most happy if you and mother could come here, and my wife Katie and all of us beg with tears that you will do so. It would be a heartfelt joy to me to be with you again, and show my gratitude to God and to you according to the fourth commandment, with the devotion and service of a good son."

Probably the best example of Martin Luther's respect for his parent's care is seen in his teaching concerning the fourth commandment. In his *Large Catechism* he insisted that honor to parents is the very foundation of all human authority. He maintained that "young people must be taught to revere their parents as representatives of God, and to remember that however lowly, poor, feeble and queer they may be, they are their own father and mother, given them by God." Being obedient to our parents is "the greatest work that we can do, next to the sublime worship of God." Furthermore, obedience is the proper expression of "gratitude for the kindness and all the good things we have received from our parents."

According to Hans and Margaret Luther, character-building and religion went hand-in-hand. Though they had a low regard for priests, they were God-fearing people, faithful in attending Mass and in saying prayers at their son's bedside. They saw God as a hard father and a stern judge; reflecting their own moods. God was terribly exacting in His demands—finally damning most of humankind to everlasting hell.

Alongside their devotion to God, they did their best not to anger the spirits that lurked everywhere about them. Typical of peasants in those times, Martin Luther's parents believed in witches, elves, angels, and demons of all kinds. They believed that devils caused misfortune, sickness, insanity, and death, while witches had the power to summon the devils. Luther's parents were firmly convinced that such things existed, and Martin never really worked himself free from such beliefs. He carried much of the superstition of his parents through all his life.

NOTE

[1]Based on Robert H. Fischer, *Luther*, Lutheran Church Press, Philadelphia, 1966, pp. 29–33.

The 475th Anniversary of Martin Luther's Coming to Wittenberg (1508)[1]

Hans Luther's ardent desire that his oldest son become a renowned lawyer was never to be fulfilled. Martin graduated from the University of Erfurt in 1505 and was preparing to study law, but the direction of his life was abruptly and radically changed. The sudden death of a friend and a narrow escape from lightning moved Luther so profoundly that the study of law was abandoned and the monastic life was embraced. In September, 1506, he took the vows of poverty, chastity and obedience, and in May of the following year he was ordained a priest.

Under the leadership of Johann von Staupitz, the

provincial vicar of the Augustinian Eremites, Erfurt monastery assumed a thoroughly medieval theological position. Much emphasis was placed upon preaching and some of its members were inclined toward mystic piety. Luther's fellow friars gave him friendly counsel but his spiritual turmoil increased. He was given the assurance that the passion of Christ had atoned for sinful man and had opened to redeemed man the gates of Paradise. Reading the German mystics, especially Tauler, gave him hope of bridging the gap between a naturally sinful soul and a righteous, omnipotent God; but the reading of a treatise by John Huss brought with it much doctrinal doubt. Luther wondered why "a man who could write so Christianly and so powerfully had been burned. . . . I shut the book and turned away with a wounded heart."

Staupitz took a fatherly interest in Luther. He advised him to put aside asceticism and give himself to a careful study of the Bible and of St. Augustine. Luther showed so much promise that Staupitz recommended him for a position on the staff of the University of Wittenberg and transferred him to the Augustinian monastery at Wittenberg. Shortly after his arrival in this Saxon town, Martin Luther assumed the post of instructor in logic and physics at the University, which had been founded by Elector Frederick, the Wise. Later, he would become the University's most famous theologian.

One day, in the course of his studies, Martin Luther was struck by a sentence in Paul's Epistle to the Romans: "the just shall live by faith" (1:17). Pondering those words, he gradually adopted the view that persons are justified—made just and saved from hell—not by good works, but only by a complete faith in Christ and in his atonement for mankind. In reading Augustine, he came upon the idea of predestination: "that God, even before cre-

7

ation, had destined some souls to salvation, the rest to hell; and that the elect had been chosen by God's free will to be saved by the divine sacrifice of Christ." These discoveries at Wittenberg in 1508 and in the following year set Luther on a course that would lead to the igniting of the Protestant Reformation less than a decade later.

Wittenberg was the northern capital of Frederick the Wise. A contemporary described it as "a poor, insignificant town, with little, old, ugly wooden houses." Luther described the town's people as "beyond measure drunken, rude and given to reveling." Theirs was the reputation of being the heaviest drinkers in Saxony, which was rated as the most drunken province of Germany. "One mile to the east", Luther once said, "civilization ends and barbarism begins." Here Luther lived for most of his remaining days.

NOTE

[1]Based on Will and Ariel Durant, *The Reformation*, Simon and Schuster, New York, 1957, pp. 343–344.

The 150th Anniversary of Hermann Garlich's Founding of the First German Evangelical Church in America, at Femme Osage, Missouri (1833)

Discovering that he did not possess in his personality the qualities required of a successful farmer, Hermann Garlichs decided to leave his farm on the banks of the Femme Osage Creek and return to Germany. His neighbors, however, whom he called "my Tecklenbergers", and a group of Germans who had settled thirty miles to the east in the vicinity of St. Charles, begged him to stay and become their pastor. For this work, Hermann Garlichs was amply qualified, except for the fact that he was not ordained.

He had received a thorough education at the universities of Gottingen, Leipzig, Bonn and Munich, through the generosity of his father, a wealthy Bremen merchant. Garlichs loved music and had some knowledge of medicine. It is also reported that he knew seven languages.

Amidst the revolutionary turmoil plaguing Germany at that time Hermann Garlichs and others had been attracted by the writings of Gottfried Duden, who had settled in Missouri. As a result, Garlichs, with a group of Westphalians of the Reformed faith, set sail for the United States of America. With some of these companions, Garlichs settled on the Femme Osage Creek, about fifty miles west of St. Louis, Missouri, in St. Charles County. Purchasing a farm six miles from Duden's home, he tried to establish himself in the new land as a farmer, but failed.

Responding to the appeal to become their pastor, Garlichs brought his German neighbors together to form the Evangelical Church at Femme Osage in 1833. The following year he organized Friedens Church at St. Charles, Missouri, where others of his friends had settled.[1] He returned to Germany only long enough to be ordained and to get married, and was soon back in Missouri, assuming his duties as the pastor of the first German Evangelical congregation to be organized in America.[2]

In 1817, sixteen years prior to the founding of the Femme Osage congregation, the United Evangelical Church of Prussia—the Church of the Prussian Union—

was called into being by the royal proclamation of King Frederick William III. This ruler decreed that henceforth the Lutheran and Reformed elements in his kingdom would work together as one communion and would be known by the name "Evangelical". He regarded this to be a most fitting way to celebrate the three hundredth anniversary of the beginning of the Protestant Reformation.

Some complained that the king had acted high-handedly. They called this new church a pawn of the state. But his action gave expression to feelings that had existed in most of the German states for some time: a longing for the union of Protestant forces.

Frederick William's action was favored by the majority of his subjects. No standard practices had existed to designate a congregation as distinctly "Lutheran" or distinctly "Reformed". Each province, large or small, had its own church administration, which was tied to the province in much the same way that our modern school system comes under state supervision. Hymnals, catechisms, and forms of worship varied from province to province, depending on the provincial government.[3] Traditional conflicts between Lutheran and Reformed confessions were disappearing in the early 19th century in Germany. Confessional particularity was undermined by Enlightenment criticism and by Pietism's emphasis upon spiritual truth, rather than on the doctrinal and ecclesiastical forms of religion.[4]

With confessional differences blurred or de-emphasized, many were asking why a union should not take place.[5] Friedrich Schleiermacher, the leading theologian of the day, advocated such a union. Lutheran and Reformed leaders found themselves drawn closer together in a common battle against rationalism.[6]

King Frederick William III was in step with the spirit

of the time when he issued his decree that brought Lutherans and Reformed together to form the "Evangelical" Church. Though Lutheran and Reformed churches continued to exist separately, the union movement soon spread beyond Prussia into Nassau, Hanau, Waldeck, Pfalz, Anhalt, Baden and Rheinhessen.[7]

As the movement spread beyond Prussia, opposition against it grew. Many who had favored the initial action of the king in 1817 thought that perhaps Frederick William III had gone too far in 1830 when he published a common book of worship—especially those who were determined to preserve and protect the purity of the Lutheran liturgy. Some Lutherans joined the Union, but others did not. Those who went their separate way were called "Old Lutherans."[8]

At the end of the seventeenth century, a strong pietist movement had arisen in Germany. The Pietists, convinced that faith is more than the possession of pure doctrine, developed a biblical and experiential theology in opposition to radical rationalism. As part of the effort to unite the Lutheran and Reformed confessions and to stem the tide of rationalism, the Pietists founded a large number of interconfessional Bible, missionary and tract societies throughout the German states. The chief mission societies were those located in Basel, Switzerland, and in Barmen, Germany.

The Evangelical Missionary Society of Basel was founded in 1815, two years before the Prussian Union. Expressing pietistic fervor, the society was opposed to all narrow confessional separations; it was not concerned about the creedal subscriptions or denominational affiliation of its mission graduates. Being "evangelical" was the Basel Society's only concern, and it refused to differentiate between Lutheran and Reformed. This society was to send out many missionaries to serve as pastors of Evangelical congregations on America's frontier.[9]

Evangelical immigrants were part of the great flood of Germans pouring into Missouri, Illinois, Indiana, Michigan, Iowa and Wisconsin. Forty thousand settled in Missouri and Illinois alone between 1830 and 1845.[10] They had come to America to escape a depressed economy and an authoritarian political life in their homeland. Many detested the ecclesiastical paternalism of the German provincial governments. They resented strict provincial control of the rites of baptism, confirmation, marriage and burial, and were strongly opposed to their clergy being state officials. For everyone who longed for freedom and wanted to escape the regimentation and official conservatism of Germany's state churches, America appeared to be a promised haven.

But who would minister to the religious needs of these tens of thousands of German immigrants? For several generations the newcomers would be using their native tongue, and the language barrier hampered the efforts of the older American churches to help. Lacking in a missionary outreach and not organized to work beyond the provincial borders, the state church in Germany was completely incapable of meeting the religious needs of those who left to live in another land.

At first, as in the case of the two groups who called Hermann Garlichs to be their pastor, the German settlers had to depend upon whatever resources they could muster for themselves and upon the leadership of lay preachers. It was not long, however, before effective support and ordained leadership was made available by Europe's voluntary missionary societies. The societies possessed the kind of resources that the frontier church needed in facing its problems. They offered a deep concern for persons and inspired workers to seek out the persons who could be helped by the church. Graduates of the Basel Missionary Society were soon arriving in America and carrying on an effective ministry among the German people on the western frontier.[11]

NOTES

1. Carl E. Schneider, *The German Church On The American Frontier*, Eden Publishing House, St. Louis, Missouri, 1939, pp. 58–59.

2. *On the Trail Of The U.C.C.*, a Historical Atlas of the United Church of Christ, compiled and edited by Carolyn E. Goddard, United Church Press, N.Y., 1981 p. 77.

3. *A History Of The Evangelical and Reformed Church*, David Dunn, et. al., The Christian Education Press, Philadelphia, 1961, pp. 148–149.

4. *History and Program Of The United Church of Christ*, United Church Press, 1978, p. 28.

5. Dunn, *op. cit.*, p. 49.

6. Ibid., p. 154.

7. *History and Program of The United Church of Christ*, ibid. pp. 28–29.

8. Dunn, *op. cit.*, p. 150.

9. Ibid., pp. 151–153.

10. *History and Program Of The United Church of Christ*, pp. 28–29.

11. Dunn, *op. cit.*, pp. 158–159.

The 150th Anniversary of Friedrich Schmid's Arrival in America (1833)

In response to a plea from Jonathan Mann to his relative, Pastor E. Josenhans in Basel, Switzerland, who was a member of the executive committee of the Basel Missionary Society, Friedrich Schmid was sent to the village of Ann Arbor, Michigan. The village had been first settled in 1825, the year that the Erie Canal was completed. By 1855, five thousand Wuertembergers from southern Germany had settled in Wahensaw County. These German immigrants were concerned about the religious future of their children. A Presbyterian Church had been established in 1829, and the Presbyterian minister was friendly toward the newcomers, but he was unable to meet their spiritual needs. This was the situation that prompted Jonathan Mann to make his appeal to Basel. Mann wrote that the Wuertembergers in Ann Arbor needed a virile young pastor to work among two hundred or more Germans who were interested in forming a congregation.

Friedrich Schmid was reared in Waldorf, not far from Stuttgart—the same area from which many of the immigrants had come.[1] He came to the Michigan Territory by steamboat from Buffalo, New York, disembarking at Detroit. The German people of Detroit persuaded Schmid to spend the weekend with them and lead a service on Sunday, August 18, 1833. The next morning he baptized several children before continuing his journey to Ann Arbor. St. John's Evangelical Church dates from that visit, although it was not formally organized until later. The present church, St. John's-St. Luke United Church of Christ, was formed in 1969, when St. Luke, organized in 1891 by people from St. John's, reunited with the parent church.

In November, 1833, Schmid formally organized the First German Evangelical Society of Scio. This became the present Bethlehem United Church of Christ in Ann Arbor. A log chapel was ready for use in December and a parish school was begun. In addition to ministering to the German settlers, Friedrich Schmid was a missionary to the Native American tribes living along the banks of the Grand River.[2]

During his ministry of more than forty years, Schmid established twenty congregations, with Ann Arbor as his home base. He "sowed the seed of church development" among the Germans in an area extending from Saginaw in the north to Monroe in the south—a distance of 119 miles—and from Detroit in the east to Lansing in the West—eighty-four miles, an area about the size of the land of Palestine.

Friedrich Schmid was the first of 288 missionaries trained by the Basel Missionary Society who would serve in America during the next century and the first of 158 who would serve congregations of the Evangelical Synod. In line with the continental meaning of the word "Evangelical", the Basel Society was especially anxious to unite Lutheran and Reformed peoples. Usually, its missionary pastors did not represent any one denomination, and the earliest German congregations in the Midwest had no denominational affiliation.

At first, Schmid did not know what to do about affiliating with a denomination. He briefly belonged to a Lutheran synod, but soon removed himself from it, unable to accept what he called their "doctrinal strife" and their "stiff and strict forms and ceremonies". Until his death, Friedrich Schmid was able to keep the congregations together in a loose federation, which he called the "Michigan Synod". Years later, they would affiliate with various Lutheran denominations and with the Evangelical Synod of North America.

In 1851, Schmid wrote a letter to Basel in which he expressed a spirit and method that was typical of most Basel missionaries:

> I for my part would like to remain faithful to the true teachings of our forefathers and to the beliefs of the Evangelical Church in which I enjoy the peace and blessing of the Lord. For nearly eighteen years, I have served in numerous congregations here with the holy Word and

sacrament, in which there are Lutheran and Reformed from the homeland, yet I have never had to experience the slightest criticism on the part of the Reformed because of my teachings or creed. As far as church practices are concerned, I maintain everything according to the Wuertemberg church, except that from early times we did not have communion wafers. If the divine truth is proclaimed in a godly and powerful manner, and the pastor lives in the strength of the gospel, then the truth-loving and truth-seeking people of both confessions can get along together through the strength of the Word, and this will occur too without any attempt to force a union. For that reason there are, I think, many in the congregations here whose parents were Reformed, but I am not certain; I do not inquire about it, for they are happy and united with and through the proclaimed Word of the cross and the holy sacraments. As far as the rigid Old Lutherans are concerned, with whom I have come into contact without learning to know them, I respect their sound teachings, but these people are mostly lacking in living faith, and for that reason there is so little love and so much harshness toward others. This rigid ceremony and this strong condemnation of others are terrible things to me. I find no good fruit here, and despite the fact that a great deal is said about church, church life and activity suffer. I could not join such a synod out of conviction.[3]

NOTES

1. *A History of the Evangelical and Reformed Church*, David Dunn, et. al.; The Christian Education Press, Philadelphia, 1961, p. 160.

2. *On The Trail of the U.C.C.*: A Historical Atlas of the United Church of Christ, compiled and edited by Carolyn E. Goddard, United Church Press, New York, p. 55.

3. Dunn, *op, cit.*, pp. 160–162.

The 125th Anniversary of The Plan For a Federative Union of the Evangelical Synods (1858)[1]

The *Kirchenverein des Westens,* the *Kirchenverein* of Ohio, and the German United Evangelical Synod of North America met together at the call of the latter at Cincinnati in 1858 to consider the possibility of a federative—not organic—union of the Synods. During the discussions, it became apparent that such a federation would not be workable, but in the conversations the *Kirchenverein des Westens* and the *Kirchenverein* of Ohio were drawn together so closely that the Ohio *Verein* decided to unite as a body with the *Kirchenverein des Westens* by joining its Eastern District at the Conference of 1857, held at Evansville, Indiana.

The German United Evangelical Synod of North America, which had initiated the plan of federative union, was torn by internal dissensions. In 1858, because of what they regarded as the domineering attitude of synodical officers—especially that of the Rev. Joseph Hartmann of St. Paul's, Chicago—ten pastors of the Eastern District from Buffalo and other towns withdrew and formed a new synod, whose name was shortened later to The German Evangelical Synod of the East. In the following year, in protest against an alleged rationalism, twelve pastors from the Western District withdrew under Hartmann's leadership from what was left of the German United Evangelical Synod of North America and became the German United Evangelical Synod of the Northwest.

Within a few years, good feelings were restored between the two new synods, cordial relationships were established with the *Kirchenverein* of the West, and the stage was set for the union that finally took place in 1872.

NOTE

1. *A History of the Evangelical and Reformed Church,* David Dunn, et, al.; The Christian Education Press, Philadelphia, 1961, pp. 202–205.

The 125th Anniversary of The Opening of the Short-Lived Marthasville College (1858)[1]

Offering a four-year course of instruction taught in both English and German, a newly dedicated college at Marthasville, Missouri, opened its doors to students in April, 1858. The cornerstone for the building had been laid more than two years earlier, in November, 1855.

Scores of colleges were being established on the western frontier at this time thus the German Evangelical Church Society of the West was engaged in what was regarded as a fashionable enterprise, though its efforts in that direction soon proved to have been in vain.

The college was preceded by the founding of the Marthasville Seminary, which had opened in 1850 with an enrollment of eight students. Whenever a seminary was founded, the urgent need for a college to serve as a preparatory school for students entering into the Christian ministry soon followed. Accordingly, it was decided to erect a college building on the seminary campus at Marthasville.

During the college's second year of existence, only eighteen students were enrolled and the highest attendance ever reached was twenty-seven. When the Civil War broke out, parents refused to send their sons into the guerrilla-infested region along the Missouri River. Only five boys enrolled for the second semester in 1862, and the decision was made not to continue. Thus, Marthasville College became a casualty of war. The casualty list of colleges in the region was high. Of the eighty-five established in Missouri, only eight survived.

1. Based on *A History of the Evangelical and Reformed Church*, David Dunn, et. al.; The Christian Education Press, Philadelphia, 1961, pp. 182–184.

The 100th Anniversary of The Dedication of Eden Seminary's Building (1883)

Though it had rained all morning and though there was no place to stand except in moisture-laden mud, a large crowd had gathered for the ceremony on October 28, 1883, when the new seminary building was to be dedicated. Those present were quite conscious of the fact that the 400th anniversary of Martin Luther's birthday was only thirteen days away and would be celebrated on November 10th. Delegates to the General Conference, meeting at St. Louis, were among those who gathered for the dedication, but many of them arrived expressed some rather negative feelings when they arrived. They had just been told in their Conference session that the new building had cost $86,700, three times the amount of money previously proposed. There were grumblings and complaints about the "inexcusable disregard of instructions". When the tour of the new facility was completed, however, and the motives of the building committee were weighed, there were no further arguments from the critics. But it would take many years to pay off the enormous debt.

19

Immediately following the union of 1872, there had been a growing demand for the removal of the theological seminary from Marthasville, Missouri, to a less secluded place. This meant the erecting of a new building at a new location. The Seminary Board admitted that there would be advantages to be gained in making such a move, but under the prevailing circumstances, the Board was not in favor of an undertaking that would put the Synod greatly in debt.

In 1880, on the floor of the General Conference there was a call for action. Some wanted the theological seminary moved to Elmhurst and a teachers' seminary established somewhere else. The motion was made and carried that the seminary board be authorized to consider all offers for a new site and, if a suitable one was found, to take steps concurrently with the officers of the synod and district presidents to remove the seminary from Marthasville.

A site was selected by the board. It was a tract slightly short of 19 acres, not far from the Evangelical Orphans Home on the St. Charles Road, and about seven miles from the courthouse in St. Louis. The new seminary was called "Eden"; the name of the nearest stop on the Wabash Railroad.

The churches of St. Louis paid for the site, and architects drew up the plans for a new building that would cost approximately $30,000. A circular letter, describing the plans and the cost, was sent to every pastor and to every congregation; along with a request that steps be taken at the district conferences to raise the necessary money. When the plan had been approved by all the districts a building committee was appointed; consisting of three laymen, four pastors, and the president of the seminary. Looking over the plans again, the Board came to the conclusion that they had not allowed for the normal growth of the seminary that was bound to come. Wouldn't it be wiser, they asked, to build big enough right away, so that it would not be necessary to build again for many years? Plans for a much larger building were accepted. The ground was broken in the fall of 1882 and the cornerstone was laid in April 1883.

NOTE

1. *A History of the Evangelical and Reformed Church,* David Dunn, et. al.; The Christian Education Press, Philadelphia, 1961, pp. 220–230.

The 100th Anniversary of John Zimmerman's Election to the Office of President of the Evangelical Synod (1883)[1]

The General Conference, meeting in St. Louis, elected John Zimmerman, pastor of Zion Church, Burlington, Iowa, to be its president; a position which he held for eighteen years. He declined re-election in 1901 when he reached the age of seventy-five.

The Synod's first president, Adolph Baltzer, had died unexpectedly in September, 1880, and had been succeeded by the vice president, Karl Seibenpfeiffer, of Rochester, New York. Seibenpfeiffer was the pastor of a large congregation and soon discovered that he was unable to take Baltzer's place as editor of *Der Friedenbote* and as manager of the denomination's publishing business. Because of a break down in his health under the strain of trying to serve both a large congregation and the Synod, Seibenpfeiffer resigned the presidency in 1882. John Zimmerman, who had been serving as vice

21

president, then assumed the duties of president, being elected officially in 1883 at the next meeting of the General Council.

In his very first report as president in 1883, Zimmerman told the General Conference that its constitutive administrative agencies were wholly inadequate, on both the district and the synodical levels. He declared that "it should be possible for the district president to make periodic visits to every pastor and congregation. It could be done by giving him an assistant—an upper-class seminary student, for instance—during the summer half year." As to the presidency of the Synod, he declared that the question of whether the next president should serve a congregation, along with the office "deserves the most serious consideration of the Synod."

The First District, which later was divided into the New York and Atlantic Districts, had strong congregations and influential pastors in Baltimore, Buffalo, and Rochester. It strongly supported Zimmerman and advocated a return to a full-time presidency in an overture to the General Conference. The Conference took the stand that "while recognizing that the combination of the synod presidency with an active pastorate presents great difficulties . . . most of these difficulties will disappear if the president will take advantage of the liberty which the constitution of the synod gives him to send written reports to districts whose conferences he does not find time to attend." Taking the whole matter very lightly, the Conference voted to make no change in the office of president.

Six years later, when the Synod now numbered 643 ministers, the General Conference finally recognized the fact that it was impossible for the president to fulfill his duties adequately while serving a church. It was voted that the president should no longer serve a church and that his salary should be fixed at $2,000 a year.

NOTE

1. Based on *A History of the Evangelical and Reformed Church*, David Dunn, et. al.; The Christian Education Press, Philadelphia, 1961, pp. 200–202.

The 100th Anniversary of The Evangelical Synod's Acceptance of the Offer of a Mission Field in India (1883)[1]

With only one dissenting vote, the Evangelical Synod of North America launched into a program of foreign missions, and a long-standing controversy within the denomination was ended abruptly.

A Committee of nine, consisting of two laymen and seven of the Synod's most respected leaders, after much deliberation, had made the following report to the General Conference of 1883:

> As strongly as your committee was convinced (with only one dissenting voice), at the beginning of our discussions, that *now* was not yet the time for the Synod to take over a mission field of its own, so little are we now able, after the discussions we have had, to advise against taking this step.
>
> Three reasons in particular impel your committee to recommend immediate action in this matter:
>
> (1) The movement within the Synod for a mission of our own has grown in spite of all objections and opposition to a force which can no longer be ignored.

(2) Acceptance of the flourishing mission offered to us in a densely populated area of India occupied by no other society will save us the costly experiments invariably connected with the opening of a new mission field.

(3) The inescapable question whether the successful completion of the new seminary building in spite of our doubts and hesitations is not God's way of telling us that in addition to our work among our own German fellow countrymen he wants to entrust a wider and more comprehensive responsibility to us.

Since your committee sees in this matter the sign of God's will for which we have been waiting for years, the committee hereby moves that the Synod take over as soon as possible the mission field offered to it by the German Evangelical Mission Society.

After a long and thorough discussion of the proposal, the eighty-eight members of the General Conference were ready to vote. It is reported that " 'God wills it!' was the overpowering conviction that swept through the assembly as the delegates voted." With only one dissenting voice, the Conference declared that the Evangelical Synod was prepared to accept the mission field in India as its own.

The German Evangelical Missionary Society in the United States, which made the offer, had been organized in 1865 by an interdenominational group of German churches, including German and Dutch Reformed, Lutheran, Moravian, Presbyterian and Evangelical congregations. In spite of its name, it had no official connection with the German Evangelical Synod of North America, but was only one of a number of German missionary societies to which the members of Evangelical Synod congregations were making contributions. The Missionary Society had been carrying on a rapidly growing work in the Central Provinces of India since 1868,

24

but was now convinced that the mission field's potential was much greater than what it could support with its limited resources. Hence, the Society made its offer to the Evangelical Synod.

The vote of the Conference in 1883 settled a question that had been plaguing the Synod for several years. The Fourth District—Missouri and southern Illinois—went on record in 1880 as favoring the right and the duty of the Evangelical Synod to take on the responsibility of a mission field of its own, and called on the next General Conference to appoint a standing committee to take the necessary steps. The Conference took no action, but referred the matter back to the districts.

Many in the Evangelical Synod who strongly favored the work of foreign missions, were opposed to the denomination's having an independent mission field. They were convinced that greater good could be done by supporting the established mission fields of the Basel, Barmen and other German Missionary Societies. Besides, did not the Synod have a moral obligation to continue to support the work of those societies to which it owed its very existence? Between 1880 and 1883 a lively debate was carried on between the proponents and opponents of an independent mission field.

With the overwhelming vote of the Synod, the issue was resolved. The formal transfer of the mission field in India from the German Evangelical Missionary Society to the Evangelical Synod took place in May, 1884.

NOTE

1. Based on *A History of the Evangelical and Reformed Church,* David Dunn, et. al.; The Christian Education Press, Philadelphia, 1961, pp. 248, 249.

The 75th Anniversary of The Publication of Julius Henry Horstmann's Hymn Translations in The Evangelical Synod's *Christian Hymns* (1908)

Thirteen translations of hymns from German to English were included in this hymnal. Three of these were incorporated into *The Hymnal* of the Evangelical and Reformed Church; published in 1941; "The Work is Thine, O Christ Our Lord", "God of Might, We Praise Thy Name", and "Wait on God, and Trust Him Through All Thy Days".[1]

J. H. Horstmann enjoyed a long literary career. From 1906 to 1935 he served as editor of *The Evangelical Herald*, the magazine of the Evangelical Synod of North America. From 1936 to 1939 he was associate editor of the Evangelical and Reformed Church's *The Messenger*. He published *Faithful Unto Death* in 1903, compiled *Evangelical Fundamentals* in 1916, and was the co-author of *Through Four Centuries* in 1938. Horstmann's writing career began when he wrote numerous "occasional poems for relatives and friends", while serving as the pastor of congregations in Indiana and Texas.

He was ordained into the Christian ministry on December 13, 1891, after receiving his education in Northwestern College (now North Central College), Elmhurst College, and Eden Theological Seminary. His father, Henry Horstmann—a lay leader—served as treasurer of the North Illinois District of the Evangelical Synod from 1874 to 1888. Julius was born in Naperville, Illinois, on March 6, 1869.[2] Along with his literary work, Horstmann was the secretary of the Commission on Church Union of the Evangelical Synod of North America from 1928 to 1934 and was co-founder of the Caroline Mission in St. Louis. He served as a member of the Mission's board of directors from 1913 to 1927.[3]

"God of Might, We Praise Thy Name"

The first really successful German version of the famous old Latin chant, *Te Deum*, appeared in the *Katholisches Gesangbuch*, published at the command of Queen Maria Theresa, in about 1774. Others had tried to produce a German translation before that time, including Martin Luther, but none of the attempts gained much popularity. Roman Catholic authorities for the most part rejected the *Gesangbuch* because of its excessive use of tunes too secular for church use, but regarded two of its hymns as having merit; including *Grosser Gott, Wir Loben Dich*. This translation of the *Te Deum* is usually attributed to Ignaz France, since he wrote forty-seven of the hymns that appeared in the *Katholisches Gesangbuch*, but his authorship has never been proven. When Father Britt compiled the collection entitled, *The Hymns of the Breviary and Missal*, he discovered that there were at that time thirty-six translations of the German version into the English language. J. H. Horstmann's translation was the one chosen for *The Hymnal* of the Evangelical and Reformed Church.[4] The following is the first stanza of that translation:

> God of might, we praise Thy name
> For Thy deeds of strength and glory,
> Heaven and earth extol Thy fame,
> And proclaim the blessed story:
> As Thou art, Thou e'er wilt be
> Unto all eternity.

"The Work is Thine, O Christ Our Lord".

This German hymn, translated by Julius H. Horstmann, was part of the rather large body of hymnic literature produced by the missionary movement that was centered at Basel, Switzerland during the first half of the 19th century. Samuel Preiswerk was requested by the students at the Basel Mission House to write a religious text for a tune then ascribed to J. Michael Hayden and used for the mass, "Hier liegt vor Deiner Majestaet." His response was the writing of two stanzas which were sung for the first time at the annual missionary festival in 1829. Preiswerk based his words on John 12:24: "Verily, verily, I say unto you, Except a grain of wheat fall into the earth and die, it abideth by itself alone; but if it die, it beareth much fruit." Horstmann's translation of Preiswerk's first stanza reads as follows:

> The work is Thine, O Christ our Lord,
>   The cause for which we stand;
> And being Thine, will overcome
>   Its foes on every hand.
> Yet grains of wheat before they grow,
> Are buried in the earth below;
> All that is old doth parish there
> To form a life both new and fair;
>   So too are we
> From self and sin made free.

Though sung at great missionary gatherings the hymn was considered too short and lacking in a definite emphasis on international missions. Count Felician von Zaremba took care of these needs by writing a third verse in which the words "Send messengers o'er land and sea" appear.[5]

"Wait on God, and Trust Him Through All Thy Days"

Fearful concerning his investments, Johann Friedrich Raeder wrote a poem that eventually became a widely-sung hymn. Armin Haeussler tells the story in *The Story of Our Hymns: The Handbook to the Hymnal of the Evangelical and Reformed Church:*

28

Johann Friedrich Raeder, cashier of a commercial concern in his native Elberfield, Germany, had saved a bit of money and invested it in indigo, a commodity much in demand, but with a market value very sensitive to the fluctuations and uncertainties of international politics. Slow and uncertain means of communication kept investors in much suspense, and in the case of Mr. Raeder created at least one entirely sleepless night. On that particular night in 1845 he turned to God in prayer and found not only mental relief, but also the kind of trust which commits all that one has and is without reservation to the Giver of every good and perfect gift. Thereupon he wrote two verses of a poem in which he expressed full confidence in the Providence which overshadows us with its sheltering care and proves itself equal to any and every human need. Later Raeder was happy to learn that his investment was safe, but he was happier still over his increased faith in a fatherly God.

Three years later Raeder's poem appeared in Wilhelm Greef's *Maennerleider;* set to a tune composed by H. A. Cesar Malan, and arranged for these words by Ludwick Erk, a brother-in-law of Raeder. The following translation of Raeder's two verses by J. H. Horstmann was included in *Christian Hymns*, 1908:[6]

Wait on God, and trust Him through all thy days;
Cast thy cares upon Him who guides all thy ways.
Do not despair; as the morning fair
Scatters fog and darkness, God removes thy care.
'Midst all thy trials, in all thy care
God remains thy faithful Friend everywhere.

Wait on God, and trust Him through all thy days;
Cast thy cares upon Him who guides all thy ways;
Perish what will, God is refuge still;
Greater than the Helper is not any ill.

Faithful, eternal Saviour and Friend,
Save my soul from evil unto the end.

NOTES

1. *The Story Of Our Hymns: The Handbook to the Hymnal of the Evangelical and Reformed Church,* Armin Haeussler, Eden Publishing House, St. Louis, Mo., 1952, p. 726.
2. Ibid., pp. 725–726.
3. Ibid., p. 1005.
4. Ibid., p. 74.
5. Ibid., pp. 298–299.
6. Ibid., p. 479.

The 75th Anniversary of The First Full Professorship in English at Eden Seminary (1908)

In September, 1908, the Rev. Samuel D. Press became the first professor to teach full time in the English language at Eden Seminary. From the time that the Evangelical Church became established in America, it was recognized by many that pastors would need to be trained to officiate and preach in English, even though English were seen as subsidiary to German.

The founders of the seminary disagreed with one another about this matter. German-born students who knew nothing of English had little opportunity to hear the language spoken in the isolated location of the Marthasville campus. Such students often graduated from the seminary with absolutely no ability to read or understand the English language. The Rev. Joseph A. Reiger, chair of the Board of Directors until his death in 1869 felt that every seminarian should be able to preach in English. Being able to do so himself, Reiger regarded it not only as necessary, but also to the advantage of the German pastor to be able to use English in all phases of his work.

English on the elementary level had been introduced into the Marthasville curriculum in 1870. At first classes were taught only by student assistants, but twenty years later, courses in practical theology and homiletics were being taught in English at Eden Seminary by competent professors.

Samuel D. Press, a graduate of Elmhurst and Eden, had spent several years studying theology in Germany. He was serving as a successful pastor in Houston, Texas, when he was called to the new English-speaking position at Eden Seminary. Eleven years later he became the seminary's president.[1]

NOTE

1. Based on *A History of the Evangelical and Reformed Church,* David Dunn, et. al., The Christian Education Press, Philadelphia, 1961, p. 232.

The 50th Anniversary of The Evangelical Synod's Approval of the Plan of Union (1933)

By the time the Synod met in 1933, the final Plan of Union had been formally and unanimously approved by the joint commissions and had been approved by the unanimous vote of the Reformed Synod at their meeting in 1932. The dream of the Rev. Samuel D. Press, President of Eden Theological Seminary, and of the Rev. John Baltzer, President General of the Evangelical Synod, were only partially realized. They, like their counter-

31

parts in the Reformed Church, had hoped that a much larger union could have been effected; but all negotiations beyond these two denominations failed to bear fruit.

During the first half of the twentieth century, the ecumenical movement was manifesting itself in great, world-encompassing meetings, beginning with the World Missionary Conference at Edinburgh in 1910. After Edinburgh, came the Stockholm Conference on Life and Work in 1925, the World Conference on Faith and Order at Lausanne in 1927, and the Jerusalem Conference in 1928. Each called for a deeper understanding of the church as the Body of Christ and invited reflection on what that meant in relations between Christian denominations. The result of these conferences was a strong desire to overcome Christianity's institutional fragmentation and a thrust toward a union of denominations in which the oneness in Christ would be more clearly realized.[1]

Press and Baltzer had returned from the Stockholm Conference with enthusiastic reports that brought forth expressions from the various districts that the "ecumenical spirit should move from mere statements of principle to their realization." The General Conference in 1925 directed its officers to "enter into negotiations with kindred communions, looking toward organic union." The Southern District, in an overture to the General Synod in 1927, proposed that an approach be made by the denomination's officers to "some other communion which in their opinion is nearest to us in doctrine and polity." The Indiana District wanted cooperation through federation and eventual union with some other denomination, and North Illinois expressed a desire "to realize the coveted unity in the spirit for which our church has ever stood."

With so much interest in union being expressed, John

Baltzer, in 1927, proclaimed as a guiding principle to be observed in any negotiations "not the personality of Luther, nor that of Calvin, but only the personality of Christ—and 'he liveth'—may, can and will give to all the basis of union in spirit." Also effective in the movement toward union were the editorials written by Julius H. Horstmann that appeared in the *Evangelical Herald*.[2]

In 1927, an unofficial meeting of Evangelical pastors and Reformed pastors was held in Baltimore, Maryland; another was held in Appelton, Wisconsin, in 1928. During the same two years, leading churchmen of the two denominations occasionally met informally.[3]

In 1926, the Reformed Commission on Closer Union reported overtures that called for entering into talks on union with the Presbyterian Church in the United States of America and the Reformed Church in America. It soon became apparent that these two denominations were not prepared to become a part of such negotiations. Under the leadership of George W. Richards, the Reformed Church's Commission on Closer Relations and Church Union began to confer with the United Brethren in Christ.[4]

In 1928, John Baltzer, President of the Evangelical Synod, appointed a Commission on Closer Relations with Other Church Bodies chaired by H. Richard Neibuhr. In July of that year, the Commission began to enter into the discussions already underway between the Reformed Church and the United Brethren. Talks moved so quickly that a union of the three denominations appeared certain.[5]

The three-party Joint Commission produced a Plan of Union, that was referred for consideration and action to the supreme judicatories of the three churches, all three of which convened in 1929. Hopes for union were running high. The Reformed Church was especially eager

33

for a reunion with the United Brethren, since the differences that had led to their division in the early 1800s had long since been overcome.[6]

Insurmountable difficulties arose among the United Brethren, however, and they withdrew from further negotiation. The Plan of Union was received by the General Synod of the Reformed Church and referred to the classes for suggestions and amendments, but the response was not as enthusiastic as that of the Evangelical Synod.

The Reformed Church still hoped for a larger union that would include the United Brethren, the Reformed Church in America, and the Presbyterian Church in the United States of America. Talks with the Evangelical Synod were temporarily suspended as the Reformed Church made a final effort to establish the kind of relations with these other bodies that might lead eventually to union. When this did not materialize, negotiations with the Evangelical Synod resumed in February 1932. The Plan of Union was approved by the Reformed Church at its General Synod in 1932, and by the Evangelical Synod at its meeting in 1933, thus setting the stage for the birth of the Evangelical and Reformed Church in Cleveland on the night of June 26, 1934.[7]

NOTES

1. *A History of the Evangelical and Reformed Church,* David Dunn, et. al., The Christian Education Press, Philadelphia, 1961, pp. 279–280.
    2. Ibid., p. 281.
    3. Ibid., pp. 281–282.
    4. Ibid., pp. 283–284.
    5. Ibid., pp. 282–284.
    6. Ibid., p. 284.
    7. Ibid., pp. 284–286.

Anniversaries of the Reformed Stream

The 450th Anniversary of Nicholas Cop's
Inaugural Speech Before the Sorbonne (1533)

On November 1, Nicholas Cop, leader of the humanist group to which John Calvin belonged, delivered an inaugural address as the newly elected rector of the University of Paris. John Calvin probably had a hand in the preparation of the speech, and as a result was forced to leave France.

The speech began with an Erasmian plea for a purified Christianity, proceeded to a Lutheran view of salvation through faith and grace, and ended with an appeal for a tolerant hearing of new religious ideas.[1] Whether or not he helped to write the speech, John Calvin was in full agreement with the views expressed.

The speech created quite a furor, and the Sorbonne erupted in anger. King Francis I called for action against the "Lutherans," while Cop and Calvin found refuge in the home of Louis du Tillet in Angoulene.[2] The Parliament began heresy proceedings against Cop—offering three hundred crowns as a reward for his capture dead or alive—but Cop managed to escape. Using assumed names, he made his way to Basel, which had become Protestant.

Calvin's friends warned him that he too was being sought, and that, if found, would be arrested. In January, 1534, Marguerite of Navarre found it necessary to intercede for him, and shortly afterwards he fled from

Paris.[3] Under an assumed name, Calvin spent some time at Poitiers. There he gathered a few like-minded persons in a cave. Behind it were the ruins of a Roman aqueduct and below it flowed a river. It is reported that once, while administering Holy Communion in the cave, he asked his congregation to pledge themselves to go out and save France for Protestantism. Keeping faith with that pledge brought several of the group to a martyr's death. Calvin returned to Paris, but was immediately forced to flee again. On his way to Strassburg, he was robbed of all that he had, but felt encouraged when he was warmly welcomed into the home of Matthew Zell, the Reformed leader of that city.[4]

NOTES

1. Will and Ariel Durant, *The Reformation*, The Story of Civilization, Part vi, Simon and Schuster, New York, 1957. p. 480

2. Williston Walker, *A History of the Christian Church*, p. 391.

3. Durant, p. 460

4. James I. Good, *The Historical Hand-book of the Reformed Church in the United States*, Philadelphia. The Heidelberg Press, 1915. p. 17.

The 400th Anniversary of The Death of Zacharias Ursinus (1583)

Zacharias Ursinus was the chief author of the Heidelberg Catechism. When he and Caspar Olevianus were directed by Elector Frederick of the Palatinate to prepare a confession of faith, each was asked to submit a plan. That of Ursinus was preferred.

Ursinus was a faithful follower of Philip Melanchthon as a student at Wittenberg. Afterwards he attended universities in Switzerland and France, where he became acquainted with John Calvin. Accused of "Philipism" and "Calvinism," Ursinus was forced to flee from Silesia to Switzerland. He became professor of theology at Heidelberg and, though not a gifted preacher, was recognized as an excellent instructor. Being a quiet man, he had few intimate friends and found his greatest joy in his studies. Not wanting to be disturbed while he worked, Ursinus placed over the door of his study an inscription in Latin which read, "Friend, whoever thou art, if thou comest to me, be brief. Either leave me soon or aid me in my labors." His contemporaries saw him as one who lived a life of prayer, which seemed to be especially pure and holy for this world. It has been reported that he never spoke an unnecessary word and yet he was loved by all who came into contact with him.

Ursinus died at the age of 49, after serving five years as professor of the Reformed Theological Seminary in Neustadt. The inscription on his monument in the church at Neustadt calls him "a great theologian, a conqueror of heresies concerning the Person of Christ and the Lord's Supper, mighty with word and pen, an acute philosopher, a wise man, and a stern instructor of youth."[1]

NOTE

1. Joseph Henry Dubbs, *Historic Manual of the Reformed Church in the United States*, Lancaster, Pa., 1885, pp. 57–60.

The 400th Anniversary of The Death of Thomas Erastus (1583)

In his *Treatise of Excommunication*, published six years after his death, Erastus set forth the important idea that

Christian princes and magistrates have the right and duty to govern the church in their dominions and to deal with violations of the moral code. This view was held firmly by Frederick, Elector of the Palatinate, and came to be known as Erastianism. Sovereigns who adopted this concept were opposed by those who argued for the separation of Church and State. In his *Treatise*, Erastus also maintained that the visible Church must be distinguished clearly from the invisible Church. The visible Church is a community based on common faith, from which no one professing that faith should be excluded.

Thomas Erastus was born Thomas Lieber in 1524 at Baden, Switzerland. He grew up in the Reformed faith, graduated from the University of Basel, and received his doctor's degree in medicine from the University of Bologna. In 1557 he became a professor at the University of Heidelberg. On two occasions—in 1559 and 1573—Erastus served as the University's rector. Lecturing on medicine, he was widely recognized as a skillful physician.

In 1560, he was asked to assist the Reformed theologian, Peter Boquinas, in a debate against the Lutheran theologian, Johann Stoessel. Erastus was so effective in debate that he won the respect of Elector Frederick, and shortly afterwards the Elector embraced the Reformed faith. Serving on the church council of the Palatinate until 1564, Erastus devoted all his energies to promoting the Reformed Church. Though most of the people of the Palatinate remained Lutheran, the policy of the Palatinate after 1566 leaned increasingly toward the Reformed bodies in Western Europe, which looked to Geneva for leadership.[1]

NOTE

1. *Masterpieces of Christian Literature in Summary Form,* edited by Frank N. Magill, Harper and Row. New York, 1963. p. 414.

The 250th Anniversary of Conrad Templeman's Letter to the Synods in Holland (1733)

Templeman, an unordained itinerant preacher, wrote a letter to the Synods of North and South Holland, on February 13, 1733, in which he told of the beginnings of the Reformed Church in the Conestoga Valley in Lancaster County. He wrote:

> The church at Chanastocka had its origin in the year 1725, with a small gathering in houses . . . with the reading of a sermon and with song and prayer, according to their High German Church Order upon all Sundays and holidays, but on account of the lack of a minister, without the administration of baptism and the Lord's Supper.
>
> Thereafter Dominie (Rev.) Boehm served them at first (1727) voluntarily at the request of the people, later after being fully ordained he administered baptism and communion to them for the space of two years (1730–1731), upon a yearly call . . . Subsequently he also established a church order (constitution) among them and the congregation chose elders, and he himself (Templeman) exercised a careful and strict supervision over them.

Conrad Templeman, who signed the letter as "Reader of the Congregation", noted that there were 55 members.[1]

NOTE

1. *History of the Classis of Lancaster of the Eastern Synod of the Reformed Church in the United States*, Edited by the Rev. Daniel G. Glass, et al., The Classis of Lancaster, New Holland, Pa., 1941, pp. 133–134.

The 150th Anniversary of The Beginning of Frederick Augustus Rauch's Work as Principal of the Classical School in York, Pennsylvania (1833)

When the Reformed seminary was moved from Carlisle to York in 1829, Professor Lewis Mayer expressed his growing concern that the students in the seminary and applicants for admission lacked scholastic preparation for theological training. In 1829 he asked the Synod "for the privilege of connecting with the seminary a literary and scientific institution in which Latin, Greek, Hebrew, natural sciences, mathematics, logic, geography, history, and composition should be taught." The request was granted and the Classical School (or "high school") of the Reformed Church was established in a building on George Street in York, Pennsylvania. Frederick Augustus Rauch was elected its principal in 1832 and began his work the following year.

Rauch was born in Hesse Darmstadt in 1806. After studying in Heidelberg, Giessen, and Marburg, he came to the United States in 1831 and settled in Easton, Pennsylvania. While Rauch was serving briefly as a Professor of German at Layette College, the Rev. Thomas Pomp was impressed by his learning and spirit and recommended that he be put in charge of the School in York.

In 1835, the Synod voted to move both the seminary and Classical School to Mercersburg, Pennsylvania. The

School was moved immediately and received its charter as Marshall College in 1836. The seminary followed in 1837.[1]

NOTE

1. David Dunn, et al., *A History of the Evangelical and Reformed Church*, The Christian Education Press, Philadelphia, 1961 pp. 67–68.
Joseph Henry Dubbs, *Historic Manual of the Reformed Church in the United States* Lancaster, Pa., 1885, pp. 285, 286.

The 150th Anniversary of The Maryland Classis' Insistence that the Reformed and Presbyterians are Different (1833)[1]

Some Presbyterians had been declaring that they and the Reformed were really one. At its meeting in 1833, the Maryland Classis refuted such claims and ordered its preachers to discuss the differences from the pulpit. As early as 1822, there had been merger talks between the Reformed and the Presbyterians. However, the committees that were appointed to explore the possibilities of closer union, met in 1828 and concluded that organic union was not possible. For several years there was an annual exchange of delegates between both bodies, but the action of the Maryland Classis brought it to an end.

NOTE

1. Based on David Dunn, et al., *A History of the Evangelical and Reformed Church*, The Christian Education Press, Philadelphia, 1961, p. 71.

The 150th Anniversary of The Death of
Samuel Weyberg (1833)[1]

Samuel Weyberg is reported to have preached the first Protestant sermon west of the Mississippi River, in 1803. Weyberg was born in Philadelphia in 1773 and was ordained in 1793. After making extensive missionary journeys, he served as a pastor in North Carolina (1795–1803) and as a pastor in Cape Girardeau, Missouri (1803–1833).

NOTE

1. Based on Joseph Henry Dubbs, *Historic Manual of the Reformed Church in the United States* Lancaster, Pa., 1885, p. 417.

The 125th Anniversary of The Death of
Isaac Baker Woodbury (1858)

Isaac Woodbury was a hard worker who, because of a break down in his health, moved to Columbia, South Carolina. On October 26, 1858, shortly after his arrival in that city, he died at the age of 39. Having had a premonition of death, he said to a friend at his bedside, "No more music for me until I am in heaven".[1] Robert Guy McCutchan, in *Our Hymnody*, comments, "Isaac Baker Woodbury has had it said of him that at the time of his death his tunes were sung by more people in America than those of any other writer."[2]

The most beloved of those tunes is *Lake Enon*, or *Mer-*

cersburg, to which Henry Harbaugh's hymn, "Jesus, I Live To Thee", is set. The tune was originally composed for Ann Steele's hymn, "While My Redeemer's Near" and first appeared in Woodbury's *The Cythara* in 1854.[3] It was also included in his *The New Lute of Zion* (1856) and *The Dayspring* (1859).

Isaac Baker Woodbury was born at Beverly, Massachusetts on October 23, 1819. As a boy he was apprenticed to a blacksmith, but his natural talents were in music. At the age of thirteen he moved to Boston where he studied music and learned to play the violin.[4] Possessing a splendid tenor voice, Woodbury went to Europe at the age of nineteen to train as a grand opera singer.[5] After achieving some success as a ballad singer, he returned to America. He became a member of the Bay State Glee Club and founded many singing schools in New England. In 1849, Isaac Woodbury moved to New York where he taught music and edited *The Musical Review* and *The Musical Pioneer*.[7] For several years he directed the music of the Rutgers Street Church, in New York City.[8]

He made a number of trips to England, and, in connection with his search for health in Europe, he became acquainted with much new music, which he incorporated into *The New Lute of Zion*, his most popular book. Concerning its contents, Woodbury wrote in the Preface, "This music is not designed for the fastidious and scientific musician whose highest delight, and perhaps sole worship, is music as an art, but for those who love to worship God in the simple song of praise."[10]

Lake Enon, or Mercersburg, is the favorite tune of the Mercersburg Academy. Set to Harbaugh's hymn, it is sung every Sunday before the sermon.[11]

NOTES

1. Armin Haeussler, *The Story of Our Hymns: The Handbook to the Hymnal of the Evangelical and Reformed Church*, Eden Publishing House, St. Louis, Mo., 1952, p. 991.
2. *Ibid.*, p. 990.
3. *Ibid.*, p. 289.
4. Albert C. Ronander and Ethel K. Porter, *Guide To The Pilgrim Hymnal*, United Church Press, Philadelphia, 1966, p. 267.
5. Haeussler *op. cit.*, p. 991.
6. Ronander and Porter *op. cit.*, p. 268.
7. Haeussler *op cit.*, p. 991.
8. Ronander and Porter *op cit.*, p. 268.
9. Ibid.
10. Haeussler *op. cit.*, p. 991.
11. *Handbook To The Hymnal*, William Chalmers Covert, editor, Presbyterian Board of Christian Education, Philadelphia, 1936. p. 268.

The 100th Anniversary of The First Official Recognition of a Women's Missionary Society in a Reformed Church (1883)

The first known congregational society for women in a Reformed Church was organized in Xenia, Ohio, in 1877, under the leadership of Rev. S. B. Yockey. The first official recognition of the organization was given by the Pittsburgh Synod in 1833. In 1887, at the General Synod at Akron, Ohio, twenty-five women representing five synods organized the Women's Missionary Society of the General Synod, with Mrs. Yockey as its president. By that time, thirty-one congregational societies, five classical societies and one synodical society (Pittsburgh) had been organized.[1]

NOTE

1. David Dunn, et al., A History of the Evangelical and Reformed Church, The Christian Education Press, Philadelphia, 1961, p. 102.

The 75th Anniversary of The Founding of Central Seminary, Dayton, Ohio (1908)

Heidelberg College, whose chief purpose was to provide classical and theological training for candidates for the ministry, was founded at Tiffin, Ohio, in 1850. During its first year of existence it enrolled 149 students. Along with its theological section, the college maintained a strong German department for some years. A number of effective German ministers for Ohio and the West received their training in that institution.

In 1908, Heidelberg Seminary was united with the Ursinus School of Theology to form the Central Seminary at Dayton, Ohio. In 1934, Central Seminary was merged with Eden Seminary in Webster Groves, Missouri.[1]

NOTE

1. David Dunn, et al., *A History of the Evangelical and Reformed Church,* The Christian Education Press, Philadelphia, 1961, p. 132.

The 75th Anniversary of The Moving of St. Paul's Orphans Home to Greenville, Pennsylvania (1908)

St. Paul's Orphans Home was established in Butler, in 1867, for orphans in western Pennsylvania. It derived its support mainly from the Synods of Ohio and Pittsburgh. In 1908 the home was moved to Greenville.

Anniversaries of the Congregational Stream

The 400th Anniversary of Robert Browne's Flight to Scotland (1583)

The Treatises in which Robert Browne expounded the principles of Congregationalism were too revolutionary to be tolerated in England. Nevertheless, numerous copies were sent across the channel from the Netherlands. Wherever they were read, they caused such a stir that the queen issued a proclamation on June 30, 1583, declaring that Robert Browne's writings were "sundry seditious, and erroneous printed Bookes and libells, tending to the deprauing of the Ecclesiastical government established within this Realme." Persons possessing copies of the treatises were ordered to surrender them and those who distributed them were charged with sedition.

When trouble arose in the Middleburg congregation, Browne had neither the ability nor the inclination to reconcile the quarreling factions. Finding himself in disagreement with his friend Robert Harrison, he decided to remove his membership from the congregation, which he had led into exile from England. Late in 1583, Browne and four or five of his followers and their families left the Netherlands and went to Scotland. The Middleburg congregation disintegrated under Harrison's leadership, with the majority of its members joining the regular English church in the city, which had the Puritan, Thomas Cartwright, as its pastor.

51

ANNIVERSARIES TO CELEBRATE

The Martyrdom of John Coppin and Elias Thacker (1583)

John Coppin and Elias Thacker were hanged on June
4 and 5, 1583, at Bury St. Edmundson. Charges of heresy
and circulating the books of Robert Browne and his co-
worker, Robert Harrison, had been brought against them.
About forty of the books were burned at the executions.[1]

NOTE

1. Williston Walker, *A History of the Congregationalist Churches in the United
States*, American Church History Series, Charles Scribner's Son's, New York,
1894, pp. 39–40.

The 375th Anniversary of The Emigration of the Scrooby Congregation to Holland (1608)[1]

Persecuted by James I, John Smyth and his Gainsborough flock emigrated to Amsterdam in 1606. Two years
later, facing much governmental opposition and many
hardships, the Scrooby congregation, under John Robinson's leadership, also emigrated to Amsterdam. Upon
their arrival, they were informed that they were barred
from any permanent settlement in the city. The city
authorities were fearful that these new arrivals would
soon be disputing with other Separatists under the leadership of Francis Johnson, Henry Ainsworth, and John
Smyth, who were already established in Amsterdam.
They were told in effect to move on, which they did in
1609, settling in Leyden.

John Smyth, who had served as a clergyman in the
Church of England, founded the Separatist congregation in Gainsborough in 1602. The congregation soon

gained many new members from the farming district outside the town. The most notable of these was William Brewster, the postmaster in the village of Scrooby on the main road from London to York.

Brewster soon began to use the Scrooby manor in a way that was not approved by the Queen or her successor. A devout man, he was driven by a serious and active concern for the country's poor and for their religious needs. People who could travel to Gainsborough were able to hear John Smyth preach, but not everyone could get there. Since Scrooby was without the services of an ordained minister, Brewster began to lead services of worship in the manor house, which were regarded as illegal. Though she tolerated the Puritans, Queen Elizabeth forbade under threat of death the meetings of any sect that refused to accept her title as Defender of the Faith.

In 1604, the Rev. John Robinson joined the Gainsborough congregation. Apparently he had been born and reared in that part of England. He entered Corpus Christi College in 1592. Upon his graduation he became a minister of the Church of England and a teacher in the college. For several years, beginning in 1600, Robinson served as a curate in the Norwich area and experienced a period of intense mental struggle. This prompted him to return to Gainsborough and join the Separatist congregation.

Shortly after he became a member it was decided— for safety and for convenience—that the church should be divided. One portion continued to meet under Smyth's guidance in Gainsborough; the other, worshipping in the manor house at Scrooby, enjoyed the ministry of Robinson and Richard Clyfton, who had been the rector in the nearby village of Babsworth.

When the Scrooby congregation decided to follow the

sister congregation to Holland in order to escape persecution, it encountered many difficulties. The English captain, whom they hired in the fall of 1607 to ferry them across the English channel, betrayed them to the magistrates. Robinson's flock was stranded, the members lost their money, and some were briefly imprisoned. The next spring another attempt was made, this time with a Dutch captain. Again they faced a number of mishaps. The longboat carrying women and children to the ship was grounded, and the captain, whose voyage could not be delayed, set off with only the men. Caught in storms, the ship was driven nearly to Norway, and the men were anxious to know what happened to their families.

This was the last attempt to emigrate as a body. From that time on, members crossed to Holland in small groups as opportunity arose, "some at one time and some at another", according to William Bradford, "[meeting] together again according to their desires with no small rejoicing." Regarding it his duty to encourage the rear guard, John Robinson was one of the last to embark from English soil.

Eleven years later, members of this group from Scrooby boarded the *Mayflower*, crossed the Atlantic Ocean, and landed at Plymouth Rock as America's "Pilgrim Fathers".

NOTE

1. Based on Williston Walker, *A History of the Congregationalist Churches in the United States* American Church History Series, Charles Scribner's Sons, New York, 1894. pp. 56–59; and Marion L. Starkey, *The Congregational Way*, Religion in America Series, ed. Charles W. Ferguson. Doubleday and Company, Inc., Garden City, New York, 1966. pp. 19–20.

The 350th Anniversary of The Arrival of The Rev. John Cotton in New England (1633)

On September 4 the sailing ship *Griffin* reached Boston, Massachusetts, with the Rev. John Cotton, the Rev. Thomas Hooker, and the Rev. Samuel Stone. The ship had left England in early July.

John Cotton had received three degrees from the University of Cambridge. In Emmanuel College, a great Puritan stronghold, he had been fellow, head lecturer, and dean. He was ordained in 1610 and two years later became vicar of St. Botolph's in Boston, Lincolnshire. After enjoying great popularity as preacher for more than twenty years, John Cotton revealed his Puritan leanings by preaching the farewell sermon to Winthrop's fleet at Southampton in 1630. One writer commented that in 1633 this able Puritan clergyman saw "the Laudian handwriting on the wall" and, to escape persecution, decided to cross the Atlantic.[1]

In mid-ocean, Mrs. Cotton gave birth to a child who was named Seaborn. The child was not baptized immediately because the father was strict on Congregational technicalities. He maintained that only an ordained minister could administer the sacraments and that his ordination in England was no longer valid since he had no congregation with him. One week after the *Griffin* reached Boston, Seaborn Cotton was baptized in Boston Church by John Wilson. This delay in baptism prompted comment and Cotton explained it. Salt water, he said, would have been suitable. What was lacking was a "settled congregation", without which "a minister hath no power to give the seal."[2]

Related events

The Appointment of William Laud as the Archbishop of Canterbury

With the support of King Charles I, Laud enforced conformity with a heavy hand. Ecclesiastically he was a strict disciplinarian, insisting on uniformity in ceremony, dress, and worship.[3] Holding views directly opposite to those of the Presbyterians and Puritans, he proposed that there be a revival of the arts in the services of the church. Steps were taken to beautify altars, pulpits, and baptismal fonts. The cross was restored to the ritual and the surplice to the priest. Laud especially offended his opposition when he ordered the communion table, which heretofor had been placed in the center of the chancel, to be put behind a railing at the eastern end of the church. Most of the changes represented a return to Elizabethan customs and laws, but the Puritans—loving simplicity—regarded the new measures as backsliding to Catholicism and a renewal of class separation between the priest and congregation. It was obvious that William Laud thought that the Roman Church was right in "surrounding religion with ceremony and in granting to the priest an aura of sanctity." Rome's offer to make Laud a cardinal appeared to the Puritans to support their criticisms, and they called him the "Forerunner of the Anti-Christ."[4]

During the five years from 1628 to 1633 that Laud spent as bishop of the strongly Puritan diocese of London, and after being elevated to the position of archbishop, he was in all respects the King's chief advisor. The country gentry of England, who were the dominant power in the House of Commons, were strongly Calvinistic in their sympathies, and Charles soon found himself at odds with them. Acting on Laud's advice in

56

1628, the King promoted Arminians to the higher offices in the church and, in order to prevent Calvinistic discussions, had a statement prefixed to the Thirty-Nine Articles that declared that no man shall "put his own sense" on any of the Articles, "but shall take it in the literal and grammatical sense". Both of these royal actions were resented by Parliament.[5]

As archbishop, William Laud was determined to remold English morals. He aroused much opposition when he levied, through the Court of High Commission, heavy fines on persons convicted of adultery. The money so received was used to repair the decaying St. Paul's Cathedral and to drive lawyers, hucksters and gossipers from its naves.[6]

The Coronation of Charles I as King of Scotland

Shortly after becoming Archbishop, William Laud journeyed with the King to Edinburgh, Scotland, where Charles was crowned Scotland's king. The Presbyterian Scots had been shocked when the King married a Catholic and extended the authority of the bishops over the presbyteries of the Kirk. In 1625, a large part of the nobility became greatly alarmed when the "Act of Revocation" was passed, revoking all grants of church or crown lands made to Scottish families since the accession of Mary Stuart.

Commenting on the coronation, the Durants wrote that Charles "allowed the bishops to carry out the ritual with the almost Catholic ceremonies of the Anglican Church: vestments, candles, altar, and crucifix. Determined to enforce their authority over the presbyteries, the Scottish bishops drew up a set of liturgical rules, which—amended and approved by the Archbishop of Canterbury—came to be known as 'Laud's Canons'. These gave the king full jurisdiction over all ecclesiastical matters, forbade assemblies of the clergy except at the king's call, restricted the right of teaching to persons licensed by a bishop, and limited ordination to candidates accepting these canons." Charles' stamp of approval was placed upon the liturgical rules, and they were made binding upon all Scottish churches. Two years later, the king named five bishops and an archbishop, John Spottiswoode, to the Privy Council of Scotland.

Presbyterian ministers protested that "half the Reformation had been annulled" and that Charles was preparing to return Britain to Rome. When petitions from all classes were sent to the king pleading with him to revoke the canons, he replied by declaring the petitions treasonable. Scotland's revolt against Charles was being kindled.[7]

The Re-issuing of James' "Declaration of Sports" by the King and Archbishop

Sanctioning games on Sunday after Sunday prayers, the *Declaration of Sports* made the Puritans very angry. For the Puritans, God was a stern judge. They emphasized "the Calvinistic conviction that most men were the 'children of wrath', doomed before birth, by the arbitrary will of a relentless diety, to everlasting hell; and they ascribed the salvation of a few 'elect' not to good works but to divine grace granted by divine whim." Regarding themselves as eternally damned, some were constantly bemoaning their everlasting fate. The Durants, in describing the Puritan life, say:

58

The humanism of the Renaissance, the lusty natural-
ism of the Elizabethans, yielded to a sense of sin, a fear
of divine vengeance, which looked upon most pleasures
as wiles of Satan and challenges to God . . . Prynne declared all embraces 'lewd', all mixed dancing 'lascivious'.
To most Puritans music, stained glass, religious images,
surplices, anointed priests were obstacles to direct communion with God. They studied the Bible with devoted
diligence and quoted its phrases in nearly every speech,
in almost every paragraph; some zealots embroidered
their clothing with Scripture texts . . . Good Puritans
prohibited the use of cosmetics and banned hair-dressing
as vanity; they earned the nickname 'Roundheads' because they cut their hair close to the head. They denounced the theater as scandalous (it was), the baiting of
bears and bulls as barbarous, the morals of the court as pagan. They condemned festival jollities, ringing bells, gathering around the Maypole, drinking healths, playing cards.

To these Puritans, the re-issuing of the *Declaration of
Sports* was especially irritating. According to their view,
no games should be allowed on the Sabbath, the day
should be devoted entirely to God and God-prescribed
rest, and the day should no longer bear the heathen
name "Sunday". Their strict observance of the Sabbath
was extended to Christmas. They were deeply disturbed
by the fact that the day of Christ's birth was celebrated
with merrymaking, dancing and games, and rightly insisted that many Christmas customs have pagan origins.
An ideal Christmas for the Puritans would be a day of
fasting and atonement.[8]

The Persecution of Ludowyc Bowyer at Laud's Command

Ludowyc Bowyer, who had charged William Laud with
being a Catholic at heart, was fined, branded, mutilated

and sentenced to prison for life. Under Laud, Puritan preachers were silenced. Clergymen who refused to accept the new ritual imposed by the Archbishop were deprived of their parishes. Writers and speakers who repeatedly criticized the ritual, who questioned the Christian creed, and who opposed the institution of bishops were to be excommunicated and were to stand in the stocks, perhaps losing their ears.

In 1628, the Puritan preacher, Alexander Leighton, admitted that he was the author of a book that called the institution of bishops anti-Christian and satanic. At Bishop Laud's instigation, Leighton

> was put in irons and was kept in solitary confinement for fifteen weeks in an unheated cell 'full of rats and mice, and open to snow and rain'. His hair fell out, his skin peeled off. He was tied to a stake and received thirty-six stripes with a heavy cord upon his naked back; he was placed in the pillory for two hours in November's frost and snow; he was branded in the face, had his nose slit and his ears cut off, and was condemned to life imprisonment.

When the Puritan, William Prynne, in *News From Ispwich* (1636), denounced Laud's bishops as servants of the Pope and the Devil, and recommended hanging for bishops, he was branded on both cheeks, his ears were cut off and he was jailed until he was freed by the Long Parliament in 1640.

Due to such oppressive measures by the King and Archbishop, many Puritans decided to follow the Separatists across the Atlantic. The Rev. John Cotton was among them.[9]

NOTES

1. H. Shelton Smith, Robert T. Handy, and Lefferts A. Loetscher, *American Christianity, An Historical Interpretation With Representative Documents*, Vol. II,

1820–1960, Charles Scribner's Sons, New York, 1963, p. 103.

2. Marion L. Starkey, *The Congregational Way*, Religion in America Series, ed. Charles W. Ferguson, Doubleday and Co. Garden City, New York, 1966. p. 57.

3. Williston Walker, *A History of the Christian Church*, Charles Scribner's Sons, New York, 1944, p. 468.

4. Will and Ariel Durant, *The Age of Reason Begins*, The Story of Civilization, Part VII, Simon and Schuster, New York, 1961, p. 189.

5. Walker, *op. cit.*, p. 468.

6. Durant, *op. cit.*, p. 189.

7. *Ibid.*, pp. 205–206.

8. *Ibid.*, pp. 190–191.

9. *Ibid.*, pp. 189–190.

The 350th Anniversary of The Arrival of the First Minister in Dover, New Hampshire (1633)

Though the colony had existed for a decade, no minister came to Dover until William Leverich arrived in 1633. In association with several English merchants, two members of the Plymouth Council—Sir Ferdinando Gorges and Captain John Mason—established two New Hampshire colonies in 1623. One, now called Rye, was at Little Harbor, at the mouth of the Pascataqua River. The other, named Dover, was located eight miles up the river. Though much money was spent on the colonies and many skilled workman from England settled in them, "the elements of power which were fitted to conquer the difficulties of the new country" were lacking, and every effort to build up the colonies ended in failure.

Through arrangements made by several Lords, a number of families from western England, of "good estates and of some account of religion", arrived in Dover in 1633. With this influx the colony began to prosper. They had brought with them a Puritan minister, William

Leverich, a Cambridge graduate, to minister to their religious needs, but his support was so meager that in two years he left.

Upon Leverich's departure, George Burdett, a shrewd and unprincipled adventurer, became the colony's religious leader. Through correspondence with Archbishop William Laud, he did his utmost to prejudice the people of England against the Massachusetts colonists, and managed to have himself appointed governor. Accused of immoral behavior, Burdett was compelled to leave the colony. Whereupon, he entered the royalist army, was captured, and died in an English prison.

After Burdett's dismissal, spiritual leadership of the community was assumed by Hanserd Knollys, who had been a learned school teacher in Gainesborough, England. Under his direction the first church in New Hampshire was organized in December, 1638.

NOTE

1. Albert E. Dunning, *Congregationalists in America: A Popular History of Their Origin, Belief, Polity, Growth and Work* J.A. Hill and Co., New York, 1894 pp. 157–158.

The 350th Anniversary of Roger William's Return to Salem (1633)[1]

For two years Roger Williams had been in Plymouth, waiting for the storm about his activities to subside. In Boston, where he had arrived on February 5, 1631, his Separatist tendencies became readily apparent, forcing him to leave the Puritan community. Graduating from Cambridge in 1627, Williams remained at the University for two more years and became linked with the Separatist cause, though he had been ordained by the Anglicans.

When asked by the Boston church to assume the ministerial responsibilities during the absence of their pastor, John Wilson, he refused. He declared that he could not serve a congregation which held fellowship with the Anglican Church. Though he held unpopular beliefs, Roger Williams was called to be the teacher of the Salem congregation. The colony's authorities quickly reacted by sending a strong letter of protest, demanding William's dismissal.

In Plymouth, Roger Williams had been received with kindness and understanding. Governor Bradford said of him that he was "a godly man and zealous, having many precious parts, but very unsettled in judgmente." He worked with some success among the Narragansett Indians and established friendships which would later prove valuable. For a time, he assisted the Rev. Ralph Smith, and it was reported that the people liked his teaching. But eventually, because of his strong views, conflict arose between him and the members.

Returning to Salem by invitation, he began to work as an assistant to the Rev. Samuel Skelton. Soon trouble broke out anew. In a treatise, written in 1633, Roger Williams had been critical of King James' patents, which conferred title to the lands of Massachusetts to the settlers. Since the land belonged to the Indians, how could James legally grant it to his subjects? The Puritans claimed that the Indians were an ungodly people and that it was just for them to be dispossessed of their territories by the new Israelites—The Puritans—whom God had led providentially to the Promised Land. Williams discredited such a concept.

What disturbed the Massachusetts authorities was that

the young theologian had attacked the charter, the very foundation of their Bible state. Williams was summoned to appear in court and gave an account of himself. The matter was dropped, but only temporarily. Soon he was lashing out against practices that seemed to him unjust—especially the interference of the civil power in religious matters and the denial of the right to vote and to hold office to persons who were not members of the established church. He also objected to compulsory attendance at religious services and to the civil tax for the support of the clergy.

NOTE

1. Based on Clifton E. Olmstead, *History of Religion in the United States*, Prentice-Hall, Englewood Cliffs, N.J., 1960. pp. 99–101.

The 350th Anniversary of The Death of William Ames (1633)

The writings of William Ames played a dominant role in the shaping of Puritan thought. His *Medulla Theologiae* became a standard textbook of Calvinist theology among the Puritans, and in his *The First Book of Divinity* he described the Church of England as "merely a collection of sovereign congregations loosely knit together as a federation." Ames argued that the local congregation had the right to call its pastor and insisted that the ordination of a minister should be held only after his election to a church. He was just as insistent, however, that the state had the right and duty to suppress all ministers and religious persuasions that did not conform to the establishment.[1]

William Ames was born of Puritan parents and studied at Christ's College, Cambridge, under William Perkins. He left England in 1610, at the age of 34, and became a preacher in the Hague, in the Netherlands. While there, he defended Calvinism against the Remonstrants and served as the secretary at the Synod of Dort in 1618. From 1622 to 1632 he served as a professor at Franeker. During that time, he wrote and published his *Of Conscience, Its Power and Cases* (1630), a treatise on Puritan ethics and casuistry. In it, he followed his teacher, William Perkins, in developing a doctrine of conscience with detailed investigation of difficult cases. According to Ames, conscience is the judgment of the practical intellect, by which a conclusion is drawn from the moral law as to one's state before God or to the moral character of one's actions. He maintained that the virtues formulated in classical philosophical ethics can properly be evaluated only by reference to the divinely revealed moral law and the evangelical doctrine of redemption and grace. He believed that moral law, summarized in the decalogue, is substantially the same as the natural law, which provides the synthesis or major premise of the syllogism of conscience. "Conscience", says William Ames, "is a man's judgment of himself according to the judgment of God of him."[2]

NOTES

1. Clifton E. Olmstead, *History of Religion in the United States,* Prentice-Hall, Englewood Cliffs, N.J., 1960. p. 63.
2. *Masterpieces of Christian Literature in Summary Form,* edited by Frank N. Magill, Harper and Row, 1963, pp. 445–449.

The 350th Anniversary of Hugh Peter's Establishment of a Fully Congregational Church at Rotterdam (1633)[1]

Since Holland was known for its religious tolerance, the Congregational exiles from England hoped to establish their Puritan ecclesiastical system there without interference. The first successful step in that direction was taken in 1621, when, under the leadership of John Forbes of Delft, the Puritans formed a classis similar to those of the French and Dutch Reformed Churches. This classis differed from that of the Reformed system in that the Puritans denied all legislative control over local congregations.

Hugh Peter graduated from Trinity College, Cambridge. When he lost his Anglican orders in 1627, he emigrated to Amsterdam. There, with the support of William Ames, he tried to settle as co-pastor of the English Church with the Rev. John Paget. His plan did not work because Paget—a former Presbyterian and now a member of the Dutch Reformed Church—was suspicious of the Congregational Puritans and refused to join their classis.

After holding two temporary positions, Hugh Peter became the pastor of the church of the merchant adventurers at Rotterdam, where he remained until 1635. There, in 1633, he fully implemented his Congregationalism. He framed a covenant that was required of all members as a condition of receiving the sacraments, and he insisted on being "called" to the congregation. Such a pattern pleased William Ames, who, in the spring of 1632, resigned from his position at Franeker and accepted a "call" as Peter's colleague, but he died shortly afterwards.

Two years later Peter was dismissed as pastor of the

Holland congregation. After a brief sojourn in England, he boarded a ship for the New World in July, 1635. Arriving in Massachusetts he was soon called to the church at Salem.

NOTE

1. Based on Smith, Handy and Loetscher, *American Christianity, An Historical Interpretation With Representative Documents*, Charles Scribner's Sons, New York, 1960. pp. 87–88.

The 350th Anniversary of The Death of Robert Browne, Founder of Congregationalism (1633)

When Browne continued to expound his Separatist views in Scotland and denied the jurisdiction of the Scottish Church over him, he was briefly jailed in 1584. By that summer, he returned to England and was imprisoned again. Through the efforts of Lord Burghley, a relative and a leading member of Queen Elizabeth' Privy Council, Browne was released.

His preaching at Northhampton led to his excommunication by the Bishop of Peterborough. Discouraged by his successive failures and with his health shattered by his trials, Robert Browne abandoned his mission. Apparently he was worn out mentally and physically. In November, 1586, he became head of a grammar school at Southwark on terms that bound him to keep peace with the establishment and submit to its rites. Five years later, through Lord Burghley's influence, Browne was made rector of Achurch-cum-Thorpe, a small Northhamptonshire village. He seems to have held that position until his death in 1633. Though outwardly conforming, Robert Browne held to his earlier convictions about the nature and polity of the church. It is reported that he was afflicted with a form of intermittenly violent insanity that led to his imprisonment for assaulting a policeman in 1631. His imprisonment lasted until his death.

The Baptists adopted Browne's Congregational polity, his recognition of the civil authority of magistrates and his denial of the validity of any baptism that is not administered on the authority of the "gathered" Church.

Robert Browne was a pioneer of two principles that have influenced decisively the religious history of English-speaking America: the voluntary principle with respect to church membership, and the principle of the separation of Church and State.[1]

NOTE

1. *Masterpieces of Christian Literature in Summary Form,* edited by Frank N. Magill, Harper and Row, 1963, pp. 404–406.

The 325th Anniversary of The Savoy Declaration (1658)

This was a revision of the Westminster Confession made by English Congregationalists meeting in the Savoy Palace in London. Though the Congregationalists generally agreed with the Westminster Confession, they concluded that some change was necessary. Some of the articles were rewritten, but care was taken to leave their doctrinal significance essentially unaltered. The revisers simply amended the phraseology here and there and removed all that was incompatible with the Congregational theories of Church government.

This declaration contains a comment about how statements of faith should be used:

> Whatever is of force or constraint in matters of this nature, causeth them to degenerate from the *name* and *nature* of *Confessions,* and turns them from being *Confessions of Faith,* into *Exactions* and *Impositions of Faith* . . . The Spirit of Christ is in himself too *free,* great and generous a Spirit, to suffer himself to be used by any human arm, to whip men into belief; he drives not, but *gently leads into all truth,* and persuades men to *dwell in the tents of like precious Faith;* which would lose of its preciousness and value, if that sparkle of freeness shone not on it.

Italics appear throughout the printing of the Savoy Declaration, a printing style that was fashionable at the time. There may be some grammatical imperfections in this statement, such as the mixing of metaphors, but herein is set forth the insistence that a statement of faith shall be used only as a testimony of faith and never as a test of faith. The Declaration states, in effect, that at no time should the church use a creed or statement of faith as a fence over which people must jump their minds before they are considered fit for church membership. According to the Savoy Declaration, a statement of faith is useful in that it indicates the direction in which the church is moving and is an expression of those beliefs most generally agreed upon.[1]

As the result of a growing agitation for religious reform, a synod was called in Massachusetts in 1679. It was decided that steps should be taken to secure a New England Confession of Faith, and a special committee was appointed. The Synod reconvened on May 12, 1680, and the committee recommended the adoption of the Savoy Declaration. No new and distinctive confession was produced. By adopting the Declaration as the standard of their faith, the New England Congregationalists indicated that they had developed no doctrinal peculiarities of their own. This action also reflected the desire of three of the most prominent members of the committee for an expression of essential unity of belief between the Congregational Church of Old England and the New. They had been in England at the time of the preparation of the Savoy Declaration twenty-two years before and were in agreement with it. No serious change was made except the substituting of the guarded expressions of the Declaration concerning the interference of magistrates in religious matters with an article that set forth more positively the authority of the state in doctrinal questions.[2]

NOTES

1. Loring D. Chase, *Words of Faith,* United Church Press, Boston and Philadelphia, 1968. p. 10.
2. William W. Sweet, *Religion in Colonial America,* Charles Scribner, New York, 1943. pp. 109, 113–114; and Williston Walker, *A History of the Congregationalist Churches in the United States,* American Church History Series, Charles Scribner's Sons, New York, 1894. pp. 187–190.

The 300 Anniversary of The Death of Roger Williams (1683)

The kind of regard that Massachusetts' authorities had for Roger Williams is reflected in the words of Cotton Mather in his *Ecclesiastical History of New England:*

In the year 1654, a certain windmill in the Low Countries, whirling round with extra-ordinary violence, by reason of a violent storm then blowing—the stone at length by its rapid motion became so intensely hot as to fire the mill, from whence the flames, being dispersed by the high winds, did set a whole town on fire. But I can tell my reader that, about twenty years before this, there was a whole country in America like to be set on fire by the rapid motion of a windmill in the head of one particular man. Know then, that about the year 1630 arrived here one Roger Williams, who being a preacher that had less light than fire in him hath by his own sad example preached unto us the danger of that evil which the apostle mentions in Romans 10:2, 'They have a zeal, but act not according to knowledge.'[1]

In July, 1635, the Puritan authorities of Massachusetts brought charges against Roger Williams, but decided not to pass sentence until he had a chance to humble himself. At the same time, the General Court put pressure on the Salem congregation by refusing to grant them title to certain lands to which they laid claim. Angry at their high-handed tactics, Williams wrote to other churches, protesting the unjust actions of the civil leaders.

In October, he was summoned for questioning and the verdict was pronounced. It read, "Whereas Mr. Roger Williams . . . hath broached and divulged diverse new and dangerous opinions against the authority of the magistrates here . . . It is therefore ordered that the said Mr. Williams shall depart out of this jurisdiction."[2] Williams was given six weeks in which to leave, but because of his poor health and the inclemency of the weather, the court agreed to postpone the banishment until spring. However, certain conditions were attached to this extension. If he stopped preaching and persuading they

71

would be lenient. He must promise not to "go about to draw others to his opinions."[3] Others, however, visited Williams in his home and found his opinions freely expressed and unchanged by the verdict.

Officers were sent to take Williams and put him on board a ship bound for England. Warned by friends, Roger Williams left home "in the bitter winter season" and made his way through the "howling wilderness" to the headwaters of Narragansett Bay. After fourteen weeks of wandering, he stumbled upon the camp of friendly Narragansett Indians and remained in their care through the winter. In the spring, he founded the colony of Providence, which he named in remembrance of God's merciful providence unto him in his distress. He was careful to purchase the land from the Indians, and the colony became a shelter for all who were "distressed in conscience"[4]. Williams was soon joined by his wife, his two small children and some friends from Salem.

In 1639, he helped John Clarke and those associated with him to found the colony of Newport and the first Baptist congregation in America. In 1647, Newport and Providence became a single colony. Though the land had been duly bought, royal recognition was still essential. Roger Williams had secured a charter for Providence in 1643, but changes in the colony and in England now required another charter. He and Clarke set sail for England in 1651. Three years later Williams returned, but Clarke spent twelve long and desperate years trying to secure a firm legal footing for the young colony. Finally, on July 8, 1663, the English Colony of Rhode Island and Providence Plantations in New England" received a royal charter.[5]

In 1644, while in England negotiating for a patent for his "Providence Plantations", Roger Williams received a copy of a treatise, written by John Cotton, in which the writer criticized a tract written in Newgate Prison by an Anabaptist. Though busily engaged in securing a patent for his colony, Williams decided to refute in writing the remarks made by Cotton. He immediately wrote and published *The Bloody Tenent of Persecution For Cause of Conscience Discussed.*

This book contained thoughts that Williams had been formulating for eight years. It was designed to refute the philosophy of church-state, which the civil and religious authorities of Massachusetts had decided upon, as well as to state the author's own views. In the first half of *The Bloody Tenent* he replied directly to Cotton's tract. The second half is Williams' attempt to rebut a document entitled *A Model of Church and Civil Power,* which the clergy of Massachusetts had sent to the people of Salem in the autumn of 1635 in an effort to show them the errors of Williams' teachings.[6]

NOTES

1. Edwin Scott Gaustad, *A Religious History of America*, Harper and Row, New York, 1966, p. 65.

2. Ibid.

3. Ibid.

4. Clifton E. Olmstead, *History of Religion in the United States*, Englewood Cliffs, N.J., Prentice-Hall, Inc., 1960, p. 101.

5. Gaustad, *op. cit.*, p. 65f.

6. *Masterpieces of Christian Literature: in Summary Form*, ed. by Frank N. Magill, Harper and Row, New York, 1963, p. 455–456.

The 300th Anniversary of The Death of John Owen (1683)[1]

In 1674 John Owen published his *Discourse Concerning the Holy Spirit*, a massive and composite work in five sections that was a major theological contribution by one of the greatest later Puritan writers. In the earlier part of his career, Owen's Puritan views were opposed by Archbishop Laud, but these same views were responsible for his rapid rise during the rule of Oliver Cromwell. By the time that the restoration of Charles II drove him into non-conformity, John Owen had become a learned scholar, a famous theologian, and a prominent public figure. During the last twenty years of his life, he wrote extensively, prompted mostly by the controversies of the period.

The value and importance of Owen's work on the Holy Spirit is significant. It is noted that, historically, his is one of the most faithful and complete reflections of the Puritan mind. The main lines of Calvinist thought are clearly present. In this book, Owen provides perhaps the only Protestant study on a major scale of one of the neglected doctrines of Christian theology. According to John Owen:

1. the doctrine of the Holy Spirit is clearly grounded in Scripture.

2. The Spirit was active at the first creation, has been revealed in power in the old and new dispensations, and is responsible for the new creation.

3. The work of the Spirit is seen in raising the believer to new life and in maintaining one in progressive holiness.

NOTE

1. Based on *Masterpieces of Christian Literature in Summary Form*, edited by Frank N. Magill, pp. 518–522.

The 275th Anniversary of The Saybrook Platform (1708)

The formulation of the Saybrook Platform and the founding of Yale College are related: Both were achieved through the efforts of the conservative element among the Connecticut ministers, with a strong backing from Cotton Mather in Massachusetts. In 1701, due mostly to a growing liberalism, Mather's influence came to an end at Harvard. In that same year, leading Connecticut ministers were urged by the conservatives in the Boston area to consider the establishment of a new college, and the Collegiate School at Saybrook was founded. Moved to New Haven in 1716, it was renamed Yale College.[1]

During the closing decades of the 17th century and the early decades of the 18th century, Connecticut lost much of its religious zeal. All attempts at religious renewal failed, and both ministers and magistrates ruefully admitted that Puritan-fostered spirituality was languishing and stagnant.

Searching for new ways to revitalize religion, the trustees of the Saybrook school, in connection with a meeting held at Guildford on March 17, 1703, drew up and issued a circular letter to Connecticut ministers, asking them to support a request that the General Assembly of the Colony recommend the adoption of the same statement of faith adopted by Massachusetts on May 12, 1680: a revision of the Savoy Declaration.[2]

The Rev. Gurdon Saltonstall of New London was elected governor of Connecticut in December, 1707. Under his influence, the Connecticut legislature issued a call on May 24,[3] for a meeting to be held at Saybrook at the time of the next Commencement—September 9, 1708—to which each church was asked to send two delegates.[4] The representatives of the churches were to come together in their various county towns on June 28, draw up tentative schemes of church government, and choose their delegates.

The Synod met in September with twelve ministers and four laymen in attendance. Their agenda was:

1. To approve the Savoy Confession as the doctrinal standard of Connecticut.

2. To adopt the rather liberal and loose-knitted "Heads of Agreement."

3. To adopt fifteen Articles, which was the "Saybrook Platform" proper.[5]

The "Heads of Agreement" were those "assented to by the United Ministers" in London and vicinity in 1691. These United Ministers were Congregationalists and Presbyterians, who, in the "Heads," had devised a plan for the union of the two denominations in the London area. Increase Mather, who was in London at the time acting as an agent for Massachusetts, played a major role in its development. The London union soon fell apart, but the "Heads of Agreement" survived and were incorporated into Connecticut's Platform. Actually it was more Congregationalist than Presbyterian, as indicated by the absence of ecclesiastical courts, which were indispensable to Presbyterianism. In the "Heads," the United Ministers had agreed that to call a pastor a local church ordinarily needed to "consult and advise with the *Pastors* of Neighboring Congregations," but at the same time "each *particular church* hath Right to chuse their own officers." This was quite acceptable in Connecticut.[6]

In 1705, an influential group of Massachusetts ministers, representing five local Associations—Boston, Weymouth, Salem, Sherborne, and Bristol—developed a plan for strengthening church discipline. Though their document got nowhere in Massachusetts, the very heart of these *Massachusetts Proposals* was embodied in the fifteen Articles of the Saybrook Platform.[7] According to the Articles, the churches in each county were to be grouped into one or more Consociations. To these Consociations, "all cases of difficult discipline within the local church where they originated should be brought" and the decision then rendered shall be considered final except in cases of great difficulty and moment.[8] If any church or individual refused to conform to the decision rendered, that church or individual would be guilty of "Scandalous Contempt." In especially difficult cases, the next neighboring Consociation should meet jointly with the Consociation that has original cognizance of the case. "Upon all occasions ecclesiaticall," including ministerial ordinations, installations and dismissals, the help of the Consociation should be sought by each church belonging to it.[10]

Each county was to have one or more Associations of ministers, with authority to examine and recommend ministerial candidates, and to ferret out and bring before councils suspected heretics and others guilty of scandalous conduct.[11]

It was further recommended that the General Association, made up of delegates from each local Association, be formed to meet annually, but its functions were not stated.

In October, the Saybrook Platform received the approval of the Connecticut legislature, with the provision that any churches allowed by the laws of Connecticut "who soberly differ or dissent from the united churches hereby established" shall not be hindered "from exercising worship and discipline in their own way, according to their conscience." The reason for this provision was that, in its May session, the legislature had passed the Toleration Act, which granted freedom of worship to dissenters on the same terms as in England, "but requiring the payment of taxes for the support of the Congregational establishment."[12]

The provisions of the Platform were implemented in February, March, and April, 1709, when Consociations and Associations were formed in various counties.[13] The paths of development of Massachusetts and Connecticut Congregationalism began to diverge.[14] The *Massachusetts Proposals* that were introduced into Connecticut brought Congregationalists into closer fellowship with the Presbyterians of the Middle Colonies, while Massachusetts increasingly developed an independent type of Congregationalism. The Saybrook Platform was an important factor in preparing the way for the adoption of the Plan of Union in 1801.

Of historical significance is the fact that the Saybrook Platform (Confession, Heads of Agreement, and Articles) was printed in one volume, in New London, in 1710. It has the distinction of being the first book published in Connecticut.[17]

NOTES

1. William Warren Sweet, *Religion in Colonial America*, Charles Scribner, New York, 1943. p. 113.

2. H. Shelton Smith, Robert T. Handy, and Leferts A. Loetscher, *American Christianity, An Historical Interpretation With Representative Documents*, Charles Scribner's Sons, New York, 1963. p. 224.

3. Williston Walker, *A History of the Congregationalist Churches in the United States*, American Church History Series, Charles Scribner's Sons, New York, 1894. p. 206.

4. Sweet, *op. cit.*, p. 114.

5. Walker, *op. cit.*, p. 207.

6. Smith, Handy and Loetscher, *op. cit.*, p. 225.

7. Ibid.

8. Walker, *op. cit.*, p. 207.

9. Smith, Handy, and Loetscher, *op. cit.*, p. 225.

10. Walker, *op. cit.*, pp. 207–208.
11. Smith, Handy, and Loetscher, *op. cit.*, p. 225.
12. Sweet, *op. cit.*, p. 115.
13. Walker, *op. cit.*, p. 208.
14. Sweet, *op. cit.*, pp. 114–115.
15. Smith, Handy, and Loetscher, *op. cit.*, p. 225.
16. Sweet, *op. cit.*, p. 114; Walker, *op. cit.*, p. 209.
17. Smith, Handy and Loetscher, *op. cit.*, p. 225.

The 225th Anniversary of The Death of Jonathan Edwards (1758)

Death came unexpectedly to Jonathan Edwards at the age of 55. During his first years at Stockbridge, he had put his theology into its final form in three great works: *An Inquiry into the Freedom of the Will* (1754), *Dissertation Concerning the Nature of True Virtue* (1754), and *Dissertation Concerning the End for Which God Created the World* (1754).[1] One of his most important writings, *The Great Christian Doctrine of Original Sin Defended* (1758), was ready for publication. But before he could write his intended masterpeice, *The History of Redemption*, he was called to succeed his recently deceased son-in-law, the first Aaron Burr, as president of New Jersey College, which later would become Princeton University. In a meeting with the trustees, Edwards vigorously insisted that he was not qualified for the office. He claimed that he was low-spirited, lacked alertness, and was unacquainted with any Greek classics except the New Testament. Nevertheless, his *Inquiry into the Freedom of the Will* had brought him renown, and the trustees were determined that he fill the position.

Packing up his books, Jonathan Edwards traveled to Princeton, and died shortly after his arrival. Cases of

smallpox had been reported and he decided to get inoculated as a precaution. Vaccination had not yet been
invented. To be inoculated meant intentionally
undergoing the disease after careful preparation and
under medical supervision, with the assurance that this
would make one immune to a more serious and unex-
pected attack. Perhaps because he had been continually
ill with fever and ague, Edwards did not survive the
inoculation. His daughter Esther was inoculated at the
same time, and she also died.[2]

On October 5, 1703, Jonathan Edwards was born at
East Windsor, Connecticut, the fifth child and the only
son among ten daughters of the Rev. Timothy Edwards,
and his wife, the daughter of Rev. Solomon Stoddard.
Both parents were deeply concerned for the liberal education and spiritual nurture of their children.[3] At the
age of ten, Jonathan revealed unusually high intelli-
gence by writing a tract on *The Nature of the Soul*.[4] In his
Notes on Natural Science, such as his observations of spi-
ders, he showed a devoted concern for empirical data,[5]
and before he entered Yale College at the age of thirteen
he possessed a knowledge of Greek, Latin, and Hebrew.[6] The permanent location of Yale was still being
determined, so part of his education was received in
Wetherfield and the other part in New Haven, where
the Rev. Samuel Johnson was his tutor.[7] By fifteen, Edwards had mastered the works of John Locke[8] and was
deeply influenced by Locke's *Essay on Human Understanding*.[9] In 1720 at the age of seventeen, he graduated
at the head of his class of ten.[10]

After studying in New Haven for two more years to
pursue his theological studies, Jonathan Edwards was
licensed to preach in 1722, and for two years he served
a congregation in New York.[11] At the age of nineteen,
he sketched out a philosophy similar to the subjective

80

idealism of Bishop George Berkley, although he was apparently unacquainted with the bishop's writings.[12] Returning to Yale, Edwards labored for two years as a tutor, at a time when tutoring was regarded as an apprenticeship for ministry.[13]

In 1727, he was ordained in Northampton as the junior colleague of his grandfather, Solomon Stoddard. When his grandfather died two years later, Jonathan Edwards assumed full ministerial responsibility in a town that was becoming the most influential in western Massachusetts and that had become well known through his grandfather's ministry.[14] In those early years at Northampton, he soon gained the reputation of loving books and abstract ideas more than pastoral evangelism. Thirteen hours of each day were spent in study.[15] In the same year that he was ordained, Edwards married Sarah Pierrepont, daughter of one of the founders of Yale.

Though he prayed as he walked in the woods, Jonathan Edwards entered Yale "unconverted", and it was only during the time he was pursuing his post-graduate studies—in 1721—that he experienced a conversion. He later described the experience in his *Personal Narrative*:

> The first instance that I remember of that sort of inward, sweet delight in God and divine things that I have lived much in since, was on reading those words, I Timothy 1:17. *Now unto the King eternal, immortal, invisible, the only wise God, be honor and glory for ever and ever. Amen.* Not long after I first began to experience these things . . . I walked abroad alone, in a solitary place in my father's pasture, for contemplation. And as I was walking there, and looking up on the sky and clouds, there came into my mind so sweet a sense of the glorious majesty and grace of God that I know not how to express. I seemed to see them both in sweet conjunction, majesty and

meekness joined together[16] . . . After this my sense of divine things gradually increased.

Jonathan Edwards became greatly disturbed by the "licentiousness" that prevailed among Northampton's youth. He wrote:

> Many of them were very much addicted to night walking, and frequenting the tavern, and lewd practices . . . It was their manner frequently to get together in conventions of both sexes for mirth and jollity, which they called frollics, and they would often spend the greater part of the night in them.

He added that many of them were "indecent in their carriage at meeting."

Edwards met with the young people in their homes and reported that when they sensed his pastoral concern, they began to improve in their behavior. He noted in 1733 that the youth had grown "observably more decent in their attendance on public worship."[17]

He became alarmed at the growing popular tendency toward Arminianism, which appeared to be breaking down the traditional emphasis on man's utter depravity. The moral level was low, and intemperance and other forms of vice were common. Edwards was convinced that the Arminian doctrine of human ability and its light regard for sin was largely responsible for undermining the Christian faith.[18] To counter the trend, he preached a series of sermons, beginning in December, 1734, in which he set forth the doctrine of justification by faith alone, exhorted to the duty of immediate repentance, and denied that any action—however good in itself—done by the "unconverted" man laid any claim upon divine justice or the promise of grace.[19]

A deep spiritual concern pervaded Northampton, and

religion became the chief topic of conversation. The people were very much stirred by the vividness with which Jonathan Edwards depicted the wrath of God, from which he urged them to flee. His preaching appealed to young and old alike, and by May, 1735, when the movement began to abate, the number of converts had grown to more than three hundred.[20] On a Sunday morning when a hundred new members were received, there was so huge a crowd that the meeting house could not hold them. Agonizing sinners thronged to the parsonage day and night seeking the pastor's help so that they too might "join the company of the saved and the rejoicing."[21] Soon the revival spread to other towns in the Connecticut Valley. Every settlement on the river was affected, and it reached to Lebanon, New Haven, Stratford and Groton. Edwards, however, limited his involvment primarily to his parish.[22]

In *A Faithful Narrative of the Surprising Work of God in the Conversion of Many Hundred Souls in Northampton, and Neighboring Towns and Villages,* he described in minute detail, yet with amazing reserve, the wondrous workings of the Spirit, confessing that they were beyond his comprehension. He perceived the revival to be "an Extraordinary dispensation of Providence" and was grateful that it was not accompanied by censorious behavior and emotional excesses. It is said of the *Narrative* that it presents "a masterly portrayal of the true Christian convert."[23] It was published in London in 1737 and was reprinted in Boston in 1738. Through it, attention of the entire Anglo-Saxon world was aroused to the American revival movement. John Wesley read it as he walked from London to Oxford. George Whitefield read it during his first visit to Georgia in 1738, and it had a decisive influence on both men.[24]

At Rev. Benjamin Colman's invitation, Whitefield arrived at Newport, Rhode Island, on September 14, 1740. Three days later he was in Boston and spent ten days preaching to huge congregations. Between December, 1740 and March, 1741, Whitefield's preaching mission was followed by that of Gilbert Tennent. By the spring and summer of 1741, the Great Awakening in New England was in full swing. Many ministers had become involved in itinerant evangelism, and it is reported their preaching was accompanied by physical demonstrations that manifested the high pitch of spiritual excitement prevailing among their hearers.[25]

At Yale's commencement exercises in 1741, Jonathan Edwards delivered his address on *The Distinguishing Marks of the Spirit of God, Applied to that uncommon Operation that has lately appeared on the Minds of many of the People of New England: With a Particular Consideration of the extraordinary Circumstances with which this Work is attended.* In it he defended some of the manifestations that were regarded as objectionable by critics of the revival, declaring them to be representative of true Christian experience.

Challenged by the Rev. Charles Chauncey of Boston, Edwards wrote in 1746 the first of his great theological works: *A Treatise Concerning Religious Affections.* It is regarded today as one of America's profoundest inquiries into the nature of religious experience.[26]

On July 8, 1741, Jonathan Edwards preached his famous sermon at Enfield, Connecticut, on the theme, *Sinners in the Hands of an Angry God.* No single sermon made more of an impression upon his hearers, though it was not typical of his preaching.[27] It was reported that "there was such a breathing of distress, and weeping, that the preacher was obliged to speak to the people and desire silence, that he might be heard." Some persons claimed that they had visions of heaven and hell

84

in which Christ showed them their name written in the Book of Life.[28]

Typically, Edwards' pulpit appearance was unassuming and his manner of preaching was mild.[29] He did not conform to the popular image of a revivalist. His sermons were tightly knit and closely reasoned expositions of theological doctrine. They were read, instead of spoken extemporaneously.[30] It has been said that "it was the message itself and the complete sincerity with which it was delivered which pierced the heart like a flaming arrow."[31]

Though Jonathan Edwards probably expected to spend his remaining years in Northampton, the congregation became increasingly dissatisfied with their minister. A case of discipline against certain young people, caught circulating "bad books", was badly handled. The "bad books" referred specifically to a manual for midwives. The pastor's methods aroused the anger of some respectable families and alienated nearly all of the town's youth.[32]

Edwards was also outspoken in his disapproval of the lax standards for church membership sanctioned by the Half-Way Covenant. The principle cause of disharmony in the congregation was his change of mind regarding who could properly receive the Lord's Supper and his opposition to the views of his own grandfather. Solomon Stoddard was in favor of admitting unconverted persons to the sacrament, convinced that this was one way to lead the sinner to a conversion experience. For Jonathan Edwards, the sacrament was not a "converting ordinance", but a "confessing ordinance" and should be restricted to professing Christians who were members of the visible church. In 1748, when he requested permission to preach a series of sermons on qualifications for admission to Holy Communion, he was firmly refused, and it was demanded that he tender his resignation.

Edwards had dedicated twenty-three years of his life to Northampton. He had made it for a time "a famous center of orthodoxy and revived spirituality". Following his farewell sermon on July 1, 1750, however, he, his wife, and their seven dependent children were expelled from the community.[33]

Jonathan Edwards then received a call from Stockbridge to serve as a missionary to the Housatonic Indians. Stockbridge, Massachusetts, was a frontier town where the Society for the Propagation of the Gospel in New England and the Bay Colony's Board of Commissioners for Indian Affairs maintained the mission.[34] Edwards had become keenly interested in foreign mission work and befriended David Brainerd, a convert of the Great Awakening. Brainerd died in Edward's home in October, 1747. After his death, Jonathan Edwards prepared the *Memoirs of Brainerd* for publication. The book did much to stimulate missionary work around the world. After reading it, Henry Martyn became the father of modern missions in India.[35]

While in Stockbridge, Edwards produced several very important theological works. One was his *Enquiry into . . . The Freedom of the Will*, published in 1754, in which he differentiated between a natural and moral ability in men. In this work he writes as an intense Calvinist, but shows that he is as keenly aware of the difficulties of the old Calvinism as he is of the shortcomings of the new Arminianism. He emphasizes the absolute sovereignty of God in conversion, as any good Calvinist would do.[36] Then he holds that, while men have a natural ability to turn to God, they lack moral ability or the inclination to do so. This determining inclination is the transforming gift to God; though its absence is no excuse for sin.[37]

In the same year, Edwards published his *Nature of True Virtue*. In it he identified goodness with being or existence. The more existence a being has the, more excellent it is. God, being infinite, has the most being— or love for being, which in its fullness is God. Therefore our greatest love must be for God. Our love for other beings ought to depend upon the degree to which they possess existence or partake of God's being.[38] God, the greatest of all beings, is justified in seeking God's own glory. Humans, by the same test, must place service to God and others before their own advantage. According to this view, sin is selfishness, and virtue is disinterested benevolence.[39]

Following are some evaluations of Jonathan Edwards and his work:

> Edwards would be remembered if he had lived out his days in a peaceful parish. In fact, his largest claim to remembrance stems from words on freedom, sin, virtue, and God's purposes, which were put to paper in remote frontier villages. His chief contribution is an enduring intellectual and spiritual reality, a monumental reconstruction of strict Reformed orthodoxy, which is remembered for its exegetical insight, its literary power and its philosophical grandeur.[40]

> Jonathan Edwards was more than the leader of a revival; he was a philosopher and theologian in his own right and one of the most brilliant America has produced. In some respects he was a Puritan mystic who loved to speak of 'sweetly conversing with Christ' or 'being wrapt and swallowed up in God.' He was never satisfied with a moralistic conception of piety. Religion to him was not so much morality as an experience of the reality of

God, a feeling of divine joy and happiness. On the other hand, he looked upon God as a sovereign ruler who, in His wrath, holds the unconverted sinner over the pit of hell. Thus in Edwards' thought we find a combination of the immanent God who illumines the heart of man, and the transcendent God who strikes down the sinner.[41]

His was . . . the keenest philosophical intellect that colonial America produced.[42]

In Edwards there was a rare combination of fervor of feeling, of almost oriental fertility of imagination, and intellectual acumen, which clothed all that he said with glowing force, while beneath his words flowed the stream of a most carefully elaborated theologic system; and all these more exalted and impulsive moods were emphasized by the influence of his wife, Sarah.[43]

NOTES

1. Ernest Sutherland Bates. *American Faith*, W. W. Norton & Company, Inc. New York, 1940, p. 213.
2. Marion L. Starkey, *The Congregational Way*, Religion in America Series, ed. Charles W. Ferguson, Doubleday & Company, Inc., Garden City, New York, 1966, p. 156.
3. Sydney E. Ahlstrom, *A Religious History of the American People*, Yale University Press, New Haven, 1972, p. 298.
4. James A. Stewart, *Jonathan Edwards: The Narrative*, Kregel Publications, Grand Rapids, Michigan, 1957.
5. Ahlstrom, *op. cit.*, p. 298.
6. Bates, *op. cit.*, p. 207.
7. Ahlstrom, *op. cit.*, p. 298.
8. Bates, *op. cit.*, p. 207.
9. Clifton E. Olmstead, *History of Religion in the United States*, Prentice-Hall, Englewood Cliffs, N.J., 1960, p. 163.
10. Stewart, *op. cit.*, p. 15.
11. Ahlstrom, *op. cit.*, p. 298.
12. Bates, *op. cit.*, p. 207.

13. Ahlstrom, *op. cit.*, p. 298.

14. *Ibid.*, p. 300.

15. Olmstead, *op. cit.*, p. 163.

16. Starkey, *op. cit.*, p. 133.

17. Winthrop S. Hudson, *Religion in America*, Scribner and Sons, New York, 1981, p. 65.

18. *Ibid.*

19. Williston Walker, *A History of the Congregationalist Churches in the United States*, American Church History Series, Charles Scribner's Sons, New York, 1894, p. 255.

20. *Ibid.*

21. William W. Sweet, *Religion in Colonial America*, Charles Scribner, New York, 1943, p. 283.

22. Walker, *op. cit.*, p. 255.

23. Ahlstrom, *op. cit.*, p. 302.

24. Hudson, *op. cit.*, p. 66.

25. Walker, *op. cit.*, pp. 256–258.

26. Ahlstrom, *op. cit.*, pp. 302–303.

27. Olmstead, *op. cit.*, p. 164.

28. Walker, *op. cit.*, p. 259.

29. Olmstead, *op. cit.*, p. 163.

30. Hudson, *op. cit.*, pp. 64–65.

31. Olmstead, *op. cit.*, p. 165.

32. *Ibid.* p. 171.

33. Ahlstrom, *op. cit.*, p. 304.

34. *Ibid.*

35. Stewart, *op. cit.*, p. 10.

36. Walker, *op. cit.*, p. 254.

37. Williston Walker, *A History of the Christian Church*, Charles Scribner's Sons, New York, 1944, p. 572.

38. Olmstead, *op. cit.*, p. 167.

39. Walker, *A History of the Christian Church*, *op. cit.*, p. 572.

40. Ahlstrom, *op. cit.*, p. 298.

41. Olmstead, *op. cit.*, p. 165–166.

42. Walker, *A History of the Christian Church*, *op. cit.*, p. 572.

43. Walker, *A History of the Congregationalist Churches*, *op. cit.*, p. 254.

The 225th Anniversary of The Death of Sarah Pierpont Edwards (1758)

Sarah left Stockbridge to join Jonathan at Princeton, but arrived too late. Her husband had died when an inoculation against small pox failed. Her piety was unwavering as she said of God, He "has made me adore His goodness that we had him so long. My God lives, and he has my heart."

She sensed that she had an important task before her; the rearing of the two orphaned Burr children. In September, however, on the way to join them in Philadelphia, she was fatally stricken with dysentery.[1] Sarah was buried beside her husband at Princeton.[2]

In 1727, after being installed as the junior colleague of his grandfather in the church in Northampton, Jonathan Edwards returned to New Haven and brought back the seventeen-year old Sarah Pierpont as his bride. For five years he had been waiting for her. Edwards was introduced to Sarah in the parsonage of her father, the Rev. James Pierpont of New Haven, when she was twelve years old. She was a great-granddaughter of Thomas Hooker, and her father helped to found Yale.[3]

The story is told that Sarah had never been accepted into full membership in her father's church because she could not name the exact date of her conversion. She had never known a time when she had not lived in radiant faith. When Sarah was thirteen, Young Edwards wrote concerning her:

> They say there is a young lady in New Haven who is loved of the Great Being who made and rules the world; and that there are certain seasons in which this Great Being . . . comes to her and fills her mind with exceeding delight and she hardly cares about anything except to meditate on Him. She has a strange sweetness in her mind and singular purity in her affections. She will sometimes go about from place to place singing sweetly, and seems to be always full of joy and pleasure, and no one knows for for what.[4]

Sarah was the mother of twelve children and the hostess for many guests in the Edwards' parsonage. Ministers traveling from one engagement to another—a practice that was quite common during the revivals of the Great Awakening—were always stopping for bed and board. It is said that "even if they came at midnight, necessitating the tumbling of children from one trundlebed to another, Sarah's hospitality never failed." One of the visiting ministers, George Whitefield, so envied Edwards' joy in his Sarah that he soon took a wife to himself.

Jonathan Edward's wife played a most influential role in the shaping of his theology.

> Edwards revered his wife, watched and recorded her mystical transports of ecstacy with awe and wonder. It must have been partly for this cause that this intellectual logician came to place a high value on emotion in religious experience. He would never neglect doctrine, but he recognized that without the quickening spirit provided by the emotions the soundest doctrine could become a dead thing.[5]

NOTES

1. Marion L. Starkey, *The Congregational Way*, Religion in America Series, ed. Charles W. Ferguson, Doubleday & Company, Inc., Garden City, New York, 1966, p. 156.

2. Sydney E. Ahlstrom, *A Religious History of the People*, Yale University Press, New Haven, 1972, p. 311.

3. Starkey, *op. cit.*, p. 134.

4. Starkey, *op. cit.*, p. 135; James A. Stewart, *Jonathan Edwards: The Narrative*, Kregel Publications, Grand Rapids, Michigan, 1957.

5. Starkey, *op. cit.*, p. 135.

The 225th Anniversary of Jonathan Edwards'
"The Great Christian Doctrine of
Original Sin Defended" (1758)

This work, which was going through the press at the time of Edwards' death, was his masterly response to the writings of John Taylor, an English Unitarian who published *The Scripture-Doctrine of Original Sin, in 1740.*

The Arminians opposed scholastic Calvinism's strong emphasis on total depravity, unconditional election, and irresistible grace. They insisted that people were morally responsible for their actions, and they upheld the necessity for persons to respond to God's redeeming work. These Arminian principles were set forth in Taylor's writings. In his essay, he argued that scripture does not teach the imputation of Adam's sin to his descendants. "Our nature is not to blame for our sin. Sin is the choice to do wrong, though nothing within man's nature compels such action."

Jonathan Edward's *Inquiry into the Freedom of the Will* and *The Doctrine of Original Sin Defended* are complementary and integrally related. Though he refutes Arminian teachings in both treatises, in the latter he bases his argument on common evidence.[1] He claims that the universal prevalence of sin is taught by experience and by Scripture. All persons are by nature corrupt at whatever stage of their existence from infancy to old age.[2] He says that his opponents are simply not facing up to the hard facts of life and that "their explanations of human wrong doing were highly superficial and grossly misleading." His appeal is to the "evidences of original sin from facts and events, as founded by observation and experience."[3]

Edwards "invited / the disbelievers in Original Sin / to a reading of history, a realistic report of village gossip, and a frank inspection of the police blotter. He left each to judge for himself . . . how far disinterested love . . . rules the world."[4] He claimed that it was irrelevant to speak of "the prevailing innocence, good nature, industry, felicity, and cheerfulness of the greater part of mankind."[5] It cannot be denied that sin and death are everywhere. Edwards then presents a long survey of biblical evidence of the doctrine of original sin.

To the Arminian argument that sins committed by morally responsible persons must be the result of free choices, Jonathan Edwards poses the question: "If their wills are in the first place as free to good as evil, what is to be ascribed to, that the world of mankind, consisting of so many millions, in so many successive generations, without consultation, all agree to exercise their freedom in favor of evil?" His answer was that the general and continuing disobedience of man shows that the cause of sin is "fixed, and that the fixed cause is *internal*, in man's nature . . ."

John Taylor regarded the imputation of Adam's sin to his descendants as unjust. No one should be held responsible for another person's wrongdoings. There were two traditional interpretations of the doctrine of imputation. One asserted that Adam's sin was transmitted through human genes: Parents pass on the guilt to their children. The other speaks of Adam as the representative of humankind: When Adam sinned, his guilt was imputed to his descendants because Adam was chosen to stand in their place.[6]

Jonathan Edwards had another interpretation. He argued for the unity of humankind in Adam as the basis for the doctrine of original sin.[7] He maintained that

> that which preserved personal identity, which makes the man of today the same being that sinned and was virtuous yesterday, is simply the constant creative activ-

ity of God, God, by a "constitution" or arrangement of things that is "arbitrary" in the sense that it depends on His will alone, sees fit to appoint that the acts and thoughts of the present shall be consciously continuous with those of the past and it is this ever-renewed creation that gives all personal identity to the individual. In a similar way God constituted the whole race one with Adam so that his sin is really theirs and they are viewed as "sinners, truly guilty and children of wrath on that account".[8]

Edwards says that "a tree, great grown and a hundred years old is one plant with the little sprout that first came out of the ground from whence it grew. So the human race, now some fifty-five hundred years old according to rabbinical reckoning, had grown from the sprout of Adam, and until redeemed by God's grace, shared his defect."[9] The section of his essay in which Jonathan Edwards explains the Adamic relation has been called "the most profound moment" of his philosophy.[10]

The principle ideas advanced in Edward's *The Great Christian Doctrine of Original Sin Defended*, according to Frank N. Magill, in *Masterpieces of Christian Literature in Summary Form*, are as follows:

1. The doctrine of original sin is the cornerstone of the Christian Gospel.

2. Unless people were totally depraved, there would be no need for the redemptive work of Christ or the scriptural requirement for a change of heart for entrance into the Kingdom of God.

3. To explain sin by asserting that it is the result of bad example or the misuse of freedom is to neglect its basic cause.

4. The universality of sin is evidence for the inherent depravity of human nature.

5. Any transgression of God's law deserves eternal pun-

ishment, and no good act can remove the damage to God's moral government.[11]

NOTES

1. *Masterpieces of Christian Literature in Summary Form,* edited by Frank N. Magill, Harper and Row, New York, 1963, pp. 602–603.

2. Williston Walker, *A History of the Congregationalist Churches in the United States,* American Church History Series, Charles Scribner's Sons, New York, 1894, p. 275.

3. *Masterpieces of Christian Literature, op. cit.,* p. 603.

4. Sydney E. Ahlstrom, *A Religious History of the American People,* Yale University Press, New Haven, 1972, p. 307.

5. *Masterpieces of Christian Literature, op. cit.,* p. 603.

6. Ibid., pp. 603–604.

7. Ahlstrom, *op. cit.,* p. 307.

8. Walker, *op. cit.,* pp. 275–276.

9. Marion L. Starkey, *The Congregational Way,* Religion in America Series, ed. Charles W. Ferguson, Doubleday & Company, Garden City, New York, 1966, p. 155.

10. Ahlstrom, *op. cit.,* p. 308.

11. *Masterpieces of Christian Literature, op. cit.,* p. 602.

The 175th Anniversary of The Founding of Andover Seminary (1808)

With Dr. Eliphalet Pearson serving as the President of the Board of Trustees and Professor of Natural Theology, and with the Rev. Leonard Woods occupying the chair of Christian Theology, Andover Theological Seminary opened its doors to receive students for the first time on September 28, 1808. Thirty-six students were enrolled that first year.[1] A very strict orthodox creed had been prepared, which every professor was required to sign and to repeat as an affirmation of faith once every five years, in order to retain his position.[2]

Andover Seminary was the result of the merging of the efforts of two groups working independently to found a theological seminary after the election of a liberal, Dr. Samuel Webber, as President of Harvard in 1806 made it appear certain that the school was lost to the evangelical churches.[3]

It all began when the Rev. Henry Ware of Hingham was elected Hollis Professor of Divinity—a position left vacant by the death of Dr. David Tappan in 1803. Mr. Hollis, a merchant of London, had given a partial endowment to Harvard to support a professor in divinity "of sound orthodox principles." Though Henry Ware had not declared himself to be a Unitarian, there were those—including the Rev. Jedediah Morse, an Overseer of the college—who were convinced that he was, and therefore ineligible to occupy the Hollis chair. When the right to question Ware concerning his theological beliefs was denied, a furor arose that was intense and bitter. Ware's appointment, followed the next year by Webber's election, convinced men like Eliphalet Pearson, Leonard Woods, and Jedediah Morse, that the attempt to bring Harvard under the control of the liberal party had succeeded.[4]

During the last two decades of the eighteenth century, King's Chapel in Boston stood alone in the promotion of Unitarianism,[5] but Unitarianism gradually gained a foothold on the Harvard campus. Years after he had visited Harvard College in 1801, Dr. Archibald Alexander, President of Hampden-Sidney College, Virginia, wrote that "even at the time of my visit all the young men of talent in Harvard were Unitarians." He had visited Dr. Buckminster in Portsmouth, New Hampshire, and reported that this "pride of Harvard" was "full of anecdotes such as were current at Cambridge, and which were mostly intended to ridicule evangelical opinions."[6]

96

David Tappan died in 1803, as did Joseph Willard, the College's president, the following year. Both were moderate Calvinists and widely respected. Strong efforts were put forth to fill the posts held by Tappan and Willard with men of Unitarian belief.[7] Jedediah Morse was equally determined that these positions should be filled with sound, orthodox men, and he launched a vigorous doctrinal debate.[8]

Jedediah Morse was the father of Samuel F. B. Morse, the inventor of the telegraph. He was born and reared in Connecticut at a time when that state had not yet been greatly exposed to the Unitarian trend. Following his graduation from Yale, Morse was called to the church at Charlestown in 1789. He joined the Boston Association and only gradually became aware of the Unitarian beliefs of many of its members. At first, Morse was tactful and on friendly terms with the Boston ministers, but then it came his turn to deliver Boston's Thursday lecture. For three successive nights, he lectured on the divinity of Christ. Though the reception was polite, Morse was convinced that there was an underlying opposition to his views and decided to withdraw from the Association. Thereupon, he quietly brought together pastors who shared his own principles and founded the Union Association. Though he remained friendly to the Boston ministers, he felt that he could no longer exchange pulpits with them because of their doctrines, which he called "Arian".

Jedediah Morse was serving on the Board of Overseers of Harvard when the Ware appointment was made. Since Harvard did not yet have a divinity school, Henry Ware would be responsible for guiding the young men in their theological studies. Morse knew of Ware's Unitarian leanings. He denounced the appointment as betraying the Calvinist faith of the founders of the "school of the prophets" and as contrary to the purpose of the Hollis chair. The governing boards of Harvard were seriously divided, but Ware's appointment was confirmed, and Samuel Webber, another liberal, was elected president, Morse had lost the struggle. Resigning from the Board of Overseers, he devoted himself to restoring orthodoxy to Massachusetts.[9]

Jedediah Morse, besides being a pastor and an Overseer of Harvard College, had gained a national reputation as America's leading geographer and had enlisted a large number of friends among the New Divinity men and moderate Calvinists. In 1805, he had published *True Reasons on Which the Election of the Hollis Professor of Divinity in Harvard College was Opposed by the Board of Overseers.* Later he founded the periodical, the *Panoplist,* for the spread and promotion of orthodox views.[10]

Eliphalet Pearson was the Professor of Hebrew and Other Oriental Languages at Harvard College and had been acting as president since Dr. Tappan's death. In protest to the appointment of Ware and the election of Webber, Eliphalet Pearson resigned and returned to Andover where formerly he had been the first principal of the Phillips Academy. Samuel and John Phillips had founded this most famous of New England academies in 1778.[11] They had imposed a strong religious character upon it, insisting that only the main doctrines of the gospel be taught. Provision was made for a fund to be used to support students who decided to pursue theological studies in connection with the academy.[12] Samuel and John Phillips dreamed that eventually their institution would have a Professorship of Divinity.

After resigning as the Academy's first principal, Pearson continued to serve as one of its trustees while he occupied the chair of Hebrew at Harvard from 1785 to 1806.[13] He returned to Andover, convinced that the loss of Harvard to the liberals demanded a strong counter-action and immediately took steps to found a theological seminary in connection with the Academy.[14]

For a while it seemed certain that two hostile theological seminaries would be erected side by side: one supported by the Old Calvinists led by Pearson and Morse, the other by the Hopkinsians—followers of Samuel Hopkins—led by Spring and Woods.[20] Through the publication of the *Panoplist,* a close friendship developed between Jedediah Morse and Leonard Woods. As arresdit, the intentions of both parties became known to each other and efforts to unite the two were made. Morse and Woods became convinced that it would be best for the two parties—in their opposition to the liberal trends at Harvard—to join their forces and produce one strong seminary. Eliphalet Pearson soon espoused the same cause, and the ultimate union was due largely to his untiring efforts.

Convinced that union was not possible, Bartlett, Brown and Norris—known as the Associate Founders—signed a constitution for the proposed seminary on August 31, 1807. It was committed to the trustees of the Phillips Academy who accepted the trust two days later. The constitution called for a test of professorial orthodoxy, requiring that each instructor should "be a man of sound and orthodox principles in Divinity according to that form of sound words of system of evangelical doctrines, drawn from the Scriptures and denominated the Westminster Assembly's Shorter Catechism."

Through the persistence of Pearson and Woods, the plan of union continued to be promoted, and, after concessions—chiefly by the Old Calvinists—union became a possibility. The Hopkinsians did not regard the Westminster Shorter Catechism a sufficient creedal test and thought it was unfair that the choice of professors should be committed unreservedly to the trustees of the Phillips Academy. During the summer of 1807, Samuel Spring and Leonard Woods prepared a creed to be used by the seminary that they planned to establish at West Newbury. It met the approval of the Founders, and it was agreed by both parties that each professor should assent to the creed that the Hopkinsians had prepared. With all hindering issues resolved, the seminary was organized in the summer of 1808.[21]

Madame Phoebe Phillips and her son, John Phillips of Andover, erected two buildings, one of which is known as Phillips Hall. Samuel Abbott gave $20,000 to found a professorship and in his will, left the seminary an additional $100,000. Bartlett, Brown and Norris gave $10,000 each, and from each of them, the seminary later received from $25,000 to $75,000. Norris, very much interested in foreign missions, contributed ten thousand silver dollars to the training of missionaries. In a letter concerning the building that he proposed to erect, Mrs. Phillips wrote, "I hope a prayer will be offered for every hod of brick and every bucket of mortar used in its erection."[22]

In *A History of the Congregationalist Churches In the United States*, Williston Walker comments that

> the inauguration of Andover Seminary was an event of prime importance in the history of Congregationalism. It was the beginning of a new era of theological education, it was the most formidable barrier erected against the spread of Unitarianism, it was a focus of missionary zeal, and its successful foundation marked the union between Old Calvinism and Edwardianism in Eastern Massachusetts, a union which averted a very serious division in the evangelical forces at a time when all their strength was needed.[23]

NOTES

1. Albert E. Dunning, *Congregationalists in America,* J.A. Hill and Co., New York, 1894, 288, 290.
2. Ibid., p. 290.
3. Sydney E. Ahlstrom, *A Religious History of the American People,* Yale University Press, New Haven, 1972, p. 394.
4. Dunning, *op. cit.,* p. 286.
5. Ahlstrom, *op. cit.,* p. 393.
6. Dunning, *op. cit.,* pp. 285–286.
7. Ahlstrom, *op. cit.,* p. 393.
8. Ibid. 394.
9. Marion L. Starkey, *The Congregational Way,* Religion in America Series, ed. Charles W. Ferguson, Doubleday & Co., Garden City, New York, 1966, pp. 179–180.
10. Ahlstrom, *op. cit.,* p. 394.
11. Dunning, *op. cit.,* pp. 286–287.
12. Ibid., p. 287.
13. Williston Walker, *A History of the Congregationalist Churches in America,* American History Series, Charles Scribner's Sons, New York, 1894, p. 348.
14. Ibid., p. 349.
15. Dunning, *op. cit.,* p. 287.
16. Walker, *op. cit.,* p. 349.
17. Dunning, *op. cit.,* p. 287.
18. Ibid.
19. Ibid.
20. Walker, *op. cit.,* p. 350.
21. Ibid., pp. 350, 351.
22. Dunning, *op. cit.,* p. 288.
23. Walker, *op. cit.,* p. 352.

The 150th Anniversary of The Founding of Oberlin College (1833)

With classrooms and dormitories still under construction, and with families of the staff thrust together in very crowded quarters,[1] instruction was begun at Oberlin College in the fall of 1833, with forty-five students in attendance, including fifteen women. The fact that the new college not only opened its doors to Negro students, but also to women, meant that a radical and revolutionary step had been taken.[2] This was the first college in the world to grant women equal advantages of education along with men.[3]

Inspired by the vision of a college dedicated to carrying out God's will, the Rev. John J. Shipherd and the Rev. Philo P. Stewart, seeking divine guidance, explored "the most godless reaches" of the Western Reserve for a possible site.[4] Shipherd had been pastor of the Presbyterian Church at Elyria, Ohio. He was born in Granville, New York, and had received his theological training under the hymnwriter, the Rev. Josiah Hopkins. Stewart was born in Sherman, Connecticut, and had been serving as a missionary for the American Board among the Choctaw Indians, but was presently living in Shipherd's household. In 1832, they conceived the idea of establishing a Christian college that would be open to men and women alike. They also dreamed of an institution that would provide an education for all who wanted it at a cost that would be within the reach of the most needy, and of an institution that ultimately would offer preparatory, normal, collegiate, and theological instruction.[5] Shipherd and Stewart planned to surround their college with a self-denying Christian community[6] in which all members would subscribe to a covenant.[7]

Early in 1833, the two ministers came upon a place in the swamp country of Lorain County, Ohio, which they were convinced had been designated by God as the proper site for their college and colony.[8] In April, the Oberlin Colony was founded.[9] It was named after Jean Frederic Oberlin, an inspired pastor of Alsace, in western Europe.[10] By fall, the college was in operation.

The new and very different ideas of the founders of

Oberlin were widely imitated, and it became "the mother of colleges in the West and South". Much of the clearing and building required for the new institution was done by the students themselves, who used the money they received to help pay for their education. The idea of a systematic, self-help policy in which students earned while they learned, originated at Oberlin. Furthermore, a chief emphasis was placed on manual labor and on "training future missionaries to cope with the rugged work demanded of them by frontier conditions". Courses in classical languages and in philosophies, however, were offered in the classical department.[11]

With its policy of admitting students regardless of color, Oberlin caused some trouble for neighboring Lane Seminary in Cincinnati. Angered by the seminary's discriminatory practice, Lane's students left—almost as a body—and walked through the woods to Oberlin, led by their Professor, Theodore Dwight Weld, an outspoken abolitionist.[12]

The charter of Oberlin College provided for a "Female Department, under the supervision of a lady", which will "furnish instruction in the useful branches taught in the best female seminaries, and its higher classes will be permitted to enjoy the privileges of such professorships in the Teachers', Collegiate, and Theological Departments, as shall best suit their sex and prospective employment."[13] Some who opposed this policy suggested that if women were to be enrolled in higher education "let it be done in nunlike seclusion and not in the promiscuous association with young men whose undergraduate misdeeds were well known." One critic of Oberlin warned that "this Amalgamation of the sexes won't do. If you live in a Powder House, you blow up once in a while." The students, however, were especially concerned about their reputations, and when one youth was caught propositioning a co-ed, he was taken aside by his classmates and given twenty-five lashes.[14]

Oberlin College was so successful in its innovative program that by the second year more than a hundred students were enrolled, with a waiting list of applicants.[15]

NOTES

1. Marion L. Starkey, *The Congregational Way*, Religion in America Series, Doubleday & Company, Garden City, New York, 1966, p. 276.

2. Ibid., p. 284.

3. Albert E. Dunning, *Congregationalists in America*, J. A. Hill & Co., New York, 1894, pp. 369, 370.

4. Starkey, *op. cit.*, p. 275.

5. Williston Walker, *A History of the Congregationalist Churches in America*, The American Church History Series, Charles Scribner's Sons, New York, 1894, p. 361.

6. Ibid.

7. Dunning, *op. cit.*, p. 369.

8. Starkey, *op. cit.*, p. 275.

9. Dunning, *op. cit.*, p. 369.

10. Starkey, *op. cit.*, p. 275.

11. Ibid.

12. Ibid., p. 276.

13. Simon Addison Bennett, *The Christian Denomination and Christian Doctrine*, The Christian Publishing Association, Dayton, Ohio, 1966, p. 42.

14. Starkey, *op. cit.*, p. 284.

15. Ibid., p. 276.

The 150th Anniversary of The Beginnings of Hartford Theological Seminary (1833)

See the 125th Anniversary of the Death of Bennet Tyler, p. 119

The 125th Anniversary of The Opening of Chicago Theological Seminary (1858)

On October 6th the first session of the faculty and students of the Chicago Theological Seminary was held. The *Congregational Herald* declared that "the morning of a new Theological day had dawned" and that it was "a proud day, not only for Chicago, but also for the Northwest". Several weeks later, the seminary's first two professors were inaugurated: the Rev. Joseph Haven as Professor of Doctrinal Theology, and the Rev. Samuel Colcord Bartlett as Professor of Biblical Literature.

Under the leadership of the Rev. Stephen Pett, the Board of Directors had planned only the organization of a junior class. In fact, they found it difficult to gather even that much of a student body together as the summer passed and the autumn opening date was approaching. It was not until May, 1858, that the Board became convinced that an autumn opening date for the new school was a real possibility. By that time, though, most college students had already selected their seminaries. Aware of this, the Board launched a vigorous recruiting program. They corresponded with sixty-six men—east and west—who had indicated that they intended to enter the Christian ministry, and invited them to apply for admission.

As yet there were no resident faculty members. But when word spread that the Chicago Theological Seminary really was going to open, five men from Andover and Union Seminaries requested and received permission to transfer to the new seminary, thus forming a senior class. "They wanted to identify themselves with the western churches and become adapted to the Spirit of the West". When the first year ended, all five received their degrees.

The dream that the Rev. Stephen Peet, minister of the Congregational Church at Batavia, Illinois, shared with the Rev. George S. F. Savage, minister of the Congregational Church, at St. Charles, more than four years earlier, had come true.

On March 14, 1854, Peet, wanting to explore an idea with his fellow minister, journeyed to St. Charles. Stephen Peet, a native of Vermont, had served churches in Green Bay and Milwaukee and had founded a large percentage of the Congregational and Presbyterian churches in Wisconsin. He had been the prime mover in the founding of Beloit College in 1846, but had been unsuccessful in an attempt to persuade the Presbyterians and Congregationalists to join their resources in the establishing of a theological seminary. George Savage was a graduate of Yale Divinity School and had been commissioned by the Home Missionary Society.

Stephen Peet dreamed of establishing a seminary in Chicago that would unite in its support all the Congregational churches on the frontier from Ohio to the Rocky Mountains. He had learned of a plan originated by some Michigan ministers that promised to be an exciting new approach to theological training. The curriculum was similar to that adopted for the training of medical students. The plan had been devised by the Rev. L. Smith Hobart, minister of the Congregational Church in Union City, Michigan. Following his graduation from Yale, Hobart served churches in Michigan for twenty years, and had instigated the formation of the General Association of Michigan's Congregational Ministers and Churches. Annually he attended a course in the University of Michigan's new medical school. Peet and Savage heartily endorsed Hobart's plan of combining academic study with summers of apprenticeship. They disagreed with him, however, in his proposal that a

106

theological department should be attached to the University of Michigan. Nor did they believe that the program should be limited to a single state.

Deciding to present the dream of a seminary at Chicago to other responsible Congregational leaders, the two Illinois ministers met two weeks later in the office of the *Congregational Herald* with four other ministers and a layman. They agreed unanimously that the time had come for a regional seminary to be established, and the plan of study originating in Michigan was strongly favored. They decided to meet again a month later and to discuss the matter with a larger group.

The Congregational General Association of Michigan meeting in the meantime, approved a plan for a theological seminary and directed its secretary to correspond with other Congregational State Associations, inviting them to co-operate in establishing the seminary in some agreed-upon place in the Northwest. At its meeting a short time later, the Iowa State Association also endorsed the idea.

A larger consultative group, headed by a layman, Philo Carpenter, with the encouragement of Peet and Savage, met on April 28, 1854, with representatives from Michigan and Iowa in attendance. A committee was appointed to arrange a convention to initiate action toward the founding of a seminary. The convention was held in Chicago on June 15, with most of the northwestern states and territories represented. It enthusiastically endorsed the resolution that "in view of the rapid growth of the west, the increased demand for ministers, the action of several ecclesiastical bodies in our connection, and the desire expressed and the plans partly matured by individuals, the time has fully come, in the providence of God, to take measures for the establishment of a Congregational Theological Seminary in the Northwest". Most of those present were under the appointment of the American Home Missionary Society.

A Committee of Twenty, headed by Stephen Peet, was given the task of preparing detailed plans—including site, curriculum and constitution—to be submitted to a still more representative convention that was to be called at the earliest convenient date. The Committee gave themselves only two months to prepare for the second convention, which was held at Plymouth Church, Chicago, on September 24, 1854, but they planned well. The convention was attended by fifty-four ministerial and twenty lay delegates from Congregational churches in Michigan, Illinois, Iowa, Wisconsin, and Missouri. For the first time, serious opposition to the plan was voiced.

Some who had not attended the previous meeting thought that the movement was premature. They cited the difficulties in founding a seminary and noted that many well-known seminaries were facing serious problems. An analysis of the reasons for the troubles experienced by these seminaries revealed that they were irrelevant to the Chicago situation.

Opponents argued further that there was a nationwide decrease in the enrollment of theological students and questioned the founding of still another seminary. Those favoring the seminary pointed out that there are ebbs and flows in the tide of candidates for the ministry. Besides, there were far from enough ministers to fill vacant pulpits on the frontier, and there was a demand for new churches to meet the needs of a fast-growing population. The new churches would need trained ministers.

Opponents complained that the base support for a seminary in the Northwest would be too weak. There were fewer than four hundred Congregational churches, and most of them were too small and too feeble to contribute much support. Statistics were presented to show that, in Illinois alone, new churches were being organized at the rate of ten a year, and, in Michigan, Congregationalism was even stronger than in Illinois. Proponents argued that "in a short time in the new cities that are sure to spring up, strong churches will be founded which would be able to absorb the product of the new seminary, as well as furnish adequate means of support."

The opponents contended that it probably would be better to cooperate in a joint venture with the Presbyterians. They were told that an overture from the Wisconsin Congregationalists to the Presbyterians for the establishing of a union seminary had been declined. It was noted that the venerable Dr. Leonard Bacon opposed the new seminary and that his word carried much weight. Bacon insisted that the eastern seminaries could educate and furnish all the ministers needed. Those favoring the new seminary replied that it might be better to close some of those eastern seminaries; claiming that, for its size, New England had too many Congregational seminaries. Only Andover and Bangor should be maintained. It was finally argued that it would be cheaper to send men east for their theological training. It was admitted that though this was true, most of the students would decide to stay in the east.

When all objections had been successfully countered, the convention elected a Board of Directors and a Board of Visitors. It also appointed committees to draft a constitution and prepare a curriculum. Fourteen of the eighteen ministers on the Board of Directors held appointments under the American Home Missionary Society. It could be claimed rightly that the new seminary had its rise in the home missionary movement, led by men of New England who, coming to the Mississippi Valley . . . found these great Christian commonwealths and planted institutions like Beloit, Olivet, Grinnell, and Carleton. The Seminary became a necessity to complete the liberal training of their ministers.

A charter was secured from the Legislature of Illinois on March 6, 1855, which stated that "the institution shall be equally open to all denominations of Christians." Since the word "Congregational" reflected denominational exclusiveness, it was dropped from the title.

The Board's chairman, Stephen Peet, and others favored "a close and self-perpetuating Board." The Rev. L. Smith Hobart spoke for others when he recommended that the Board of Directors be elected by the Congregational General Association. Both of these ideas were rejected, and the suggestion to put the seminary directly under the watch and control of the churches was adopted. Objections were voiced but the convention concluded that "there is more safety in leaving the power and control with the living, active body of Christ than anywhere else"—that is, with the individual Congregational churches. The constitution provided for a triennial convention; a gathering of "delegates from each of the Congregational Churches, and of all Congregational ministers who are employed in preaching in these churches, or who are members of the same." The official business of this convention, meeting every three years, was the election of the seminary's Board of Directors and Board of Visitors.

The Committee on Curriculum considered Hobart's idea: a course of theological education that combines theory and practice, modeled on a plan that appeared to be operating very successfully in medical schools. This concept had played a large role in the drive to

110

establish a new seminary "which should not merely meet the needs of ministers on the frontier, but meet that need in a novel way, by providing a new kind of theological education." The members of the committee were thoroughly indoctrinated with Hobart's scheme. In their deliberations, they explored both the advantages and the disadvantages of the traditional pattern. They concluded that Andover, Bangor, and Yale had done commendable work in raising the standards of ministerial training, but decided that most of their graduates were prepared only to serve in staid New England parishes, not on the frontier. A scholarly ministry was not rejected and there was no attempt to endorse the familiar frontier formula of substituting evangelical zeal for sound learning. According to the committee, the problems confronting the world at the time demanded "the ripest scholarship, the highest culture, and the most divine wisdom possible." It was concluded that "the traditional theological curriculum needed radical overhauling in terms not of subject matter but of methods and aims of teaching."

The decision was made to combine two kinds of theological education into a single program. The first was an apprenticeship training under a parish pastor—the method generally in use during the last half of the eighteenth century. The other was that followed by the theological seminaries since early in the nineteenth century: There was to be a lecture term of twenty-eight to thirty weeks extending from September to April, followed by a month's vacation and a reading term of twelve or thirteen weeks. During the reading term, the student was expected to pursue a course of reading recommended by the faculty. Priority during the term was to be given to the student's apprenticeship or internship under a pastor selected by himself and approved by the faculty. In addition to supervising his reading, this pastor would initiate the student into "the inside of a minister's life—to learn what are the pastor's hopes and anxieties about his Church, Sabbath-school, prayer-meeting and choir,—to go around with the pastor, and withal exercise himself, in pastoral visitation,—to see how this experienced pastor demeans himself in families visited by sickness and death,—how he warns the careless, gains the disaffected, wins the shy, and guides the inquiring,—how he marks out work for all classes in his Church, secures their cooperation, and thereby developes their graces,—in fine how by methods which no lectures on pastoral theology can unfold, he brings the forces of the gospel into work in private and social life."

One of the student's assignments would be to conduct under the pastor's supervision "the prayer meeting, receiving afterwards suggestions about this most difficult, delicate and hopeful part of the pastor's work." During the second reading term, the student would occasionally preach for the pastor, "acquiring not merely the theory but the art of public address, learning to preach by preaching, as only he can." At the end of each reading term the pastor with whom the student resided was required to submit a certificate of approval for the student to the faculty. With regard to the lecture term, the committee on the curriculum recommended no experimentation.

The committee was surprised that this combination program of theological education had not been introduced earlier. Certainly in other fields of education theory and practice had been linked together. "How nonsensical it would have been 'to educate farmers away from farms, mechanics away from shops, merchants away from marts of trade, lawyers without the details of the office and the contests of the courtroom, and physicians without clinical practice.' "

Now came the critical task of selecting a faculty for the new institution. The Board recognized that the seminary's "first instructors, more perhaps than any others, would give tone to its spirit, and set in operation influences which would be felt for ages to come." The task would not be easy. The Board had committed themselves to "work some improvement in the method of theological education" and were looking for men who would not simply copy existing forms of academic life. The new seminary required professors "in sympathy with its peculiarities, who can do a work which, in the precise shape of it here requisite, has not hitherto been done." After a long process in which they experienced a number of setbacks, the Board gave its approval to two men; the Rev. Joseph Haven and the Rev. Samuel Colcord Bartlett.

Following his graduation from Amherst College and Andover Theological Seminary, Joseph Haven spent ten years in New England as a parish pastor. For seven years he had taught a course on Mental and Moral Philosophy and had become a strong exponent of the popular Scottish philosophy, "Common Sense", which held that all knowledge must be based on principles that are self evident.

At his inauguration as Professor of Doctrinal Theology, Haven received his "charge" from the Rev. H. D. Kitchell, president of the Board of Directors, who characterized the theological stance of the new seminary as open-minded. "We hold you," he declared, "to no school in Theology or Philosophy, we have come to this faith by way of Geneva and New England, and the way we love well. But we hold you not to Calvin, or even to New England. We too have the Word which alone is sure, and to us also the inspiration of the Almighty who

113

give wisdom." Haven responded in a similar vein when he delivered his inaugural address, entitled "Theology as a Science: Its Dignity and Value". In the address he posed a series of rhetorical questions and said, "Was, then the science of theology complete as it came from the hands of Augustine, or of Calvin, of Luther, of Owen or Howe?" Haven suggested that there may have been a little progress made "even since the days of Edwards."

Samuel Bartlett, a graduate of Dartmouth College and Andover Theological Seminary, was deeply influenced by the writings of Carlyle and Coleridge. After teaching philosophy and rhetoric at Western Reserve College from 1845 to 1852, Bartlett served as a parish pastor—first in the church in Manchester, New Hampshire and then in the New England Congregational Church, Chicago.

He was widely known for his polemic against Universalism, which was becoming increasing popular at the time. The title of his inaugural address as the Professor in Biblical Literature, "Study of God's Word in the Original Tongues", indicated clearly that though Chicago Theological Seminary was located on the frontier, there would be no modifying or relaxing of the standards of classical learning deemed essential to the training of a minister.

The Rev. Franklin Woodbury Fisk joined the faculty the following year as the Professor of Homiletics. In his inaugural address, "The Forces of the Pulpit and Their Relation To Its Power", Fisk "gave expression in ringing and prophetic tone to what would become a dominant tradition at the Seminary, a concern for social order and justice."[1]

NOTE

1. A condensation of pages 1–30 of *No Ivory Tower; The Story of The Chicago Theological Seminary*, by Arthur Cushmann McGiffert, Jr., 1965.

114

The 125th Anniversary of The Death of Nathaniel W. Taylor (1858)

Nathaniel Taylor was the real architect of the "New Haven Theology", which had been founded by his beloved teacher, Timothy Dwight, President of Yale.[1] As such, Nathaniel W. Taylor became a central figure in a theological controversy, waged within the Congregational churches during the second quarter of the nineteenth century, which led to the founding of Hartford Theological Seminary.

Many Congregational clergymen, under the leadership of Timothy Dwight and Lyman Beecher, deliberately had adopted revivalistic methods. In doing so, they modified certain tenents of Calvinism in such a way that others became afraid that these clergymen were abandoning a sound theological position. A doctrine hotly debated was the doctrine of native depravity. According to strict Calvinism, all persons were by nature totally depraved, and the election of some to salvation and others to damnation was entirely in the hands of the sovereign God. Strict Calvinists argued that, inasmuch as God is infinitely good and wise, even the damnation of sinners ultimately served the purposes of glorifying God and promoting the greatest good of being in general. Moderate Calvinists, on the other hand, argued that sinners are punished because they have freely chosen evil. According to them, if the just and sovereign God punishes the sinner, this in itself indicates that the sinner indeed has free will.

Early in his career, Nathaniel W. Taylor moved toward the moderate position.[2] He was born in New Milford, Connecticut, in 1786, and graduated from Yale in 1807. At Yale he came under the strong influence of his theology professor, President Timothy Dwight. While a

115

student, Taylor served as an amanuensis for Dwight,[3] whose eyesight was poor,[4] and an intimate relationship developed between the two men. Taylor also assisted Lyman Beecher in his various campaigns.[5]

After serving as the minister of the Center Church in New Haven from 1812 to 1822, Taylor was invited to become the Dwight Professor of Didactic Theology in the newly organized Yale Divinity School[6]—a position he held until his death in 1858.

Central to Taylor's theological views was the insistence that no one becomes depraved except by one's own act, for the sinfulness of the human race does not pertain to human nature as such. As free, rational, moral, and creative agents, people are not part of the system of nature—at least not as a passive and determined part.[7] The moral choices of people are so connected with the total life-style or personality they have developed, that in any given situation their choice will appear certain or predictable from God's point of view, though a person has full power of contrary choice at all times. This "certainty," yet "with power to the contrary," makes it possible for God to be sovereign and humans to be dependent while individual persons are perfectly unforced in their actions.[8] Sin is a willful disobedience to known law. It flows out of a natural bias to sin and is expressed in an actual sinful act; but that bias, disposition, or capacity to sin is not in itself sinful.[9] Sin is in the sinning, Taylor maintained, and the only thing "original" about it is that it is universal. Though sin is inevitable, it is not, even as Jonathan Edwards himself maintained in his later years, causally necessary. Humankind always has had, in Taylor's famous phrase, "Power to the contrary".[10]

Everyone has the ability to choose aright—even the sinner—if one is aroused to that action by a proper appeal to one's mental capacities. Taylor claimed that a proper appeal can be made to self-love; since the highest form of self-love—the pursuit of highest happiness—could never be inconsistent with the choice of what is best for the universe: namely, benevolence.

Taylor further held that while a person possesses the needed natural power to change one's character so as to express a complete, undivided love toward God, it is certain that one will not turn from God-lacking, self-centered purposes unless one is led by God's Spirit to do so. Yet, when one is induced by the Spirit to act in God-intended ways, one acts without coercion.[11]

He further maintained that in a system in which the free action of the creature is permitted, God is unable to prevent sin. We must be allowed to sin or not to sin. Such a system of freedom is to be preferred to one in which God would forcibly prevent sin by allowing no freedom to the creature. Though God may not be able to prevent sin in a system of freedom, sin can be curbed, according to Taylor, by a person's being open to the guidance of God's Spirit to resist temptation.

Taylor's theological views won the general approval of his colleagues at Yale and came to be known as the "New Haven Theology".[12] Since it was necessary to maintain a united front of Calvinists against their enemies—especially the Unitarians—the widening internal differences among Calvinist leaders were deliberately prevented from surfacing. The strict Edwardeans, however, became increasingly troubled, and when it became apparent that Unitarianism was safely contained, they decided that it was time to allow the deeper doctrinal issues within the denomination to emerge into the open.

On July 30, 1826, Professor Eleazer T. Fitch tried to answer questions raised by the conservatives by stating the New Haven position forcefully. Fitch and the New

Haven Theology were vigorously attacked by the conservative press and pulpit. Nathaniel Taylor decided that, regardless of controversy, it would be best to state forthrightly the correctness of the New Haven views. This he did before a gathering of Connecticut Congregational clergymen, in the Yale Chapel, on September 10, 1828, when he delivered the annual *Concio ad Clerum*, "Advice To The Clergy". He had chosen as his text Ephesians 2:3, "And were by nature the children of wrath."[13] In this, his most famous of sermons, he set forth fully his views on sin and of its non-preventibility by divine power.[14] He tried to explain what moral depravity involved, declaring that it was our own act, consisting in a free choice of some object rather than God, but it was "by nature," since it was consistent with our nature to choose.[15]

This sermon immediately aroused heated discussion. Many of the more conservative Edwardeans of Connecticut had been suspicious of Taylor ever since the time he assumed his position in the Divinity School. Now they were convinced that the professor had made a serious departure from New England Calvinism. He was tending toward Arminianism in his denial of the full sovereignty of God. His opponents were greatly disturbed by his views concerning the nature and preventibility of sin, and especially by his theory of self-love as a motive of conversion.[16]

Nathaniel W. Taylor was especially critical of the Rev. Leonard Woods and claimed that Woods' argument against Henry Ware had set back the orthodox cause fifty years. According to Sydney E. Ahlstrom, in *A Religious History of the American People*, Taylor, unlike Woods, "was consciously formulating a reasonable revival theology that could prosper in the democratic ethos of Jacksonian America." As Taylor's theological views gradually gained acceptance, "revivals came to be understood less as the 'mighty acts of God' than as the achievement of preachers who won the consent of sinners."[17]

NOTES

1. Sydney E. Ahlstrom, *A Religious History of the American People,* Yale University Press, New Haven and London, 1972, p. 419.

2. H. Shelton Smith, Robert T. Handy, and Lefferts A. Loetscher, *American Christianity: An Historical Interpretation With Representative Documents,* Volume II, 1820–1960, Charles Scribner's Sons, New York, 1963, p. 28.

3. Williston Walker, *A History Of the Congregationalist Churches in the United States,* The American Church History Series, Charles Scribner's Sons, New York, 1894, p. 355.

4. Ahlstrom, *op. cit.,* p. 419.

5. Smith, Handy, and Loetcher, *op. cit.,* p. 29.

6. Ibid.

7. Ahlstrom, *op. cit.,* p. 420.

8. Walker, *op. cit.,* p. 356.

9. Ibid.

10. Ahlstrom, *op. cit.,* p. 420.

11. Walker, *op. cit.,* p. 356.

12. Ibid., p. 357.

13. Walker, *op. cit.,* p. 357; Smith, Handy, and Loetcher, *op. cit.,* p. 29.

14. Walker, *op. cit.,* p. 357.

15. Smith, Handy, and Loetcher, *op. cit.,* p. 29. Taylor's sermon had two major points. Smith, Handy, and Loetcher present the text of the first point in brief, but the second one in full. The main body of the sermon was followed by a series of "Remarks" which related the view of moral depravity as defended to the theological controversies then raging. Only the final remark, forming the conclusion to the whole sermon, is included in the book by Smith, Handy and Loetcher, *op. cit.,* pp. 29–36.

16. Walker, *op. cit.,* p. 357.

17. Ahlstrom, *op. cit.,* p. 420.

The 125th Anniversary of The Death of
The Rev. Bennet Tyler (1858)

Bennet Tyler died the same year as Nathaniel Taylor. Though other men had opposed Taylor's theological views as vigorously as he did, Bennet Tyler in the forefront of the opposition—made possible the popular name given to the internal squabble of the Congregationalists that eventually led to the founding of Hartford Theological Seminary: the "Tyler-Taylor Controversy".[1]

Leonard Woods, at whom Nathaniel Taylor's criticism was to some extent aimed, turned from his battle with the Unitarians and lashed out against the Yale Divinity School professor. Shortly afterwards, he was joined by Bennet Tyler and the "Tyler-Taylor Controversy" became a common topic of conversation throughout New England.[2]

Tyler was born in Middlebury, Connecticut, in 1783, and graduated from Yale in 1804. After serving as pastor of the church in South Britain, Connecticut, he became president of Dartmouth College, a position he held from 1822 to 1828. Leaving Dartmouth, he became pastor of Second Church in Portland, Maine. During the summer of 1829, Bennet Tyler visited Connecticut and "collected all the pamphlets that had been published" concerning the New Haven Theology. He then recorded that after a "careful examination of this literature" he became thoroughly convinced that "the New Haven brethren had adopted opinions which were erroneous and of dangerous tendency."[3] During that summer he began to correspond with Nathaniel W. Taylor and protested the views set forth in Taylor's *Concio ad Clerum*.[4] The opening volley of Tyler's public attack on Taylor came in an address he made in December, 1829.

A heated debate continued for two or three years, resulting in the formation of two distinct groups of Congregationalists in Connecticut. It is significant to note that discussions were going on at the same time in the Presbyterian Church that resulted in the division of that denomination into "old School" and "New School" fac-

120

tions in 1837. The Presbyterian discussions no doubt influenced the debate raging among the Congregationalists.

The first step in organizing an opposition to the New Haven Theology apparently took place on October 12, 1831, when some Connecticut ministers met at Norwich and organized a "Doctrinal Tract Society". The movement grew during the following year. Then, late in 1832, prompted by the Rev. Nathan Perkins of West Hartford and by the Rev. Joseph Harvey, an invitation was extended to all the associations of the State —and to a few in Western Massachusetts—to send two pastors each to a meeting to be held in Hartford, on January 8, 1833. Only about twenty ministers attended.

At the invitation of a committee chosen at the Hartford gathering, however, a convention of thirty-six ministers with conservative leanings met on September 10, 1833, in a little schoolhouse in East Windsor, Connecticut. Two days of deliberation resulted in the formation of a voluntary association of ministers: the "Connecticut Pastoral Union". The association adopted a conservatively Edwardean—though not extreme—creed, based on a draught that had been submitted to the meeting at Hartford the previous January. In it, the New Haven views were particularly opposed.[5]

Dissatisfaction with Yale had grown so strong that the Pastoral Union founded the Theological Institute of Connecticut as a counter-seminary[6] with their creed as its doctrinal test. The new seminary, located at East Windsor Hill, formally opened on May 13, 1834,[7] with Bennet Tyler as its President and Professor of Theology. Sydney E. Ahlstrom comments about Tyler that "here until his death he sought to build a bastion of what he thought was unrevised and uncompromised Edwardseanism."[8]

121

The name of the institution was later changed to the Hartford Theological Seminary.

NOTES

1. Williston Walker, *A History Of The Congregationalist Churches in the United States*, the American Church History Series, Charles Scribner's Sons, New York, 1894, p. 358.
2. Sydney E. Ahlstrom, *A Religious History of the American People*, Yale University Press, New Haven and London, 1972, p. 420.
3. Walker, *op. cit.*, p. 358.
4. Ahlstrom, *op. cit.*, p. 420.
5. Walker, *op. cit.*, pp. 358–359.
6. Ahlstrom, *op. cit.*, p. 420.
7. Walker, *op. cit.*, p. 360.
8. Ahlstrom, *op. cit.*, p. 420.

The 125th Anniversary of The Publication of "Nature And The Supernatural", by Horace Bushnell (1858)

In this book, according to Sidney E. Ahlstrom,

Bushnell set forth his defense of religion and the Christian faith in comprehensive terms, unfolding a total view of the cosmos. Although he guards himself from pantheism, protects the special historical significance of Christ (still with small stress on his humanity), and recognizes the reality of miracles and spiritual gifts in New Testament times and his own, in this work Bushnell exhibits his most radical innovation: his very untraditional use of the word "supernatural". For him this category includes all that has life, every aspect of reality which is not caught up in the mechanical chain of cause and effect. In such a view, nature and supernature are consubstantial and interfused; man by definition participates in supernatural life, while (conversely) God is asserted to be immanent in nature. Taken together, nature and the supernatural constitute "The one system of God."[1]

Horace Bushnell was born near Litchfield, Connecticut, in 1802, and graduated from Yale in 1827. During the next several years he was a teacher, a journalist, a student of law, and a tutor at Yale,[2] until a kind of conversion experience led him to enter Yale Divinity School in 1831.[3] At the time of his graduation in 1833, the school's professor of Systematic Theology, The Rev. Nathaniel W. Taylor, was at the height of his fame.[4] Bushnell was much influenced by Taylor and became an advocate of the New Haven Theology. Later, however, he confessed that he was much more influenced by Samuel Coleridge's *Aids to Reflection* and Friedrich Schleiermacher's comments on the Trinity. These transformed his entire view of Christianity.[5]

He became pastor of North Church, Hartford, Connecticut, which he served for twenty-six years until ill-health compelled his resignation in 1859.[6] It was a time when Calvinism had lost its greatest advocates and when the champions of Unitarianism and transcendentalism occupied the center of the theological stage. Taylor had made Horace Bushnell conscious of the need to mediate between Calvinism and the increasingly popular "liberal" theology.[7]

Bushnell's first and most famous work was *Christian Nurture* (1847). In it he dealt with the problem of original sin, provided an escape from revivalism, and established the foundation stone for a new approach to religious education.[8]

In 1848, he was invited to deliver theological addresses at Yale, Harvard, and Andover. Adding a "Preliminary Dissertation on the Nature of Language, as Related to Thought and Spirit", he published the addresses in 1849 under the title, *God In Christ*. The preliminary dissertation was very controversial. In it, Horace Bushnell insisted that verbal communication is essentially evocative, symbolic, and social in narure. He rendered the appeal to scriptural and creedal statements impossible and "robbed language of the precision which dogmaticians and heresy hunters had assumed it possessed."

Horace Bushnell's views on the Trinity, the Divinity of Christ, and the Atonement were also controversial. Clearly he found it difficult to assert Christ's real humanity. The book aroused quite a furor. In his old age, Bennet Tyler turned from his assaults against Taylor, and lashed out vigorously against this new source of error. Bushnell's fellow ministers in Hartford became increasingly reluctant to exchange pulpits with him and a heresy trial seemed imminent. It was averted only when Bushnell's own congregation, in support of him, withdrew from the consociation. As years passed, some of Horace Bushnell's theological views changed, becoming more and more traditional.[9]

Sidney E. Ahlstrom, who refers to Bushnell as the American Schleiermacher,[10] notes that "the unity and coherence of his thought is one of the factors that contributed most to the steady expansion of his influence, which was large—larger perhaps than that of any liberal theologian in American religious history." On the "new" geology, Darwin's views of evolution, women's rights, and slavery, his views were decidedly conservative. "Yet," according to Ahlstrom, "his adoption of romantic notions of process and development facilitated an accomodation of evolutionary thought and opened into the Social Gospel of Washington Gladden. . . . His broad antisectarianism, his emphasis on religious experience, his flexible view of dogma, and his eloquent optimism— all made him truly 'the father of American religious liberalism' ".[11]

NOTES

1. Syndney E. Ahlstrom, *A Religious History of the American People*, Yale University Press: New Haven and London, 1972, p. 612.
2. Williston Walker, *A History of the Congregationalist Churches in the United States*, American Church History Series, Charles Scribner's Sons, New York, 1894, p. 365.
3. Ahlstrom, *op. cit.*, p. 610.
4. Walker, *op. cit.*, p. 365.
5. Ahlstrom, *op. cit.*, p. 610.
6. Walker, *op. cit.*, p. 365.
7. *Masterpieces of Christian Literature:* In Summary Form, edited by Frank N. Magill, Harper & Row, Publishers; New York, Evanston and London, 1963, p. 716.
8. Ahlstrom, *op. cit.*, p. 610.
9. Ibid., pp. 610–611.
10. Ibid., p. 610.
11. Ibid., p. 613.

The 125th Anniversary of The Publication of the Sabbath Book Hymnal (1858)

This hymnal, edited by Edward Amasa Park, Austin Phelps, and Lowell Mason, is sometimes called the Andover Sabbath Hymn Book, because its preface is dated, "Andover, Mass., Sept. 1850". Parks and Phelps were both professors at the Andover Seminary. An invitation was extended to Ray Palmer and Horatius Bonar to contribute translations and original hymns for this collection.[2]

NOTES

1. *The Hymnal 1940 Companion,* The Protestant Episcopal Church, The Church Pension Fund, New York, 1951, p. 300.

2. Albert E. Dunning, *Congregationalists in America,* J. A. Hill & Co., New York, 1894, p. 486.

The 125th Anniversary of Ray Palmer's Translation of "Jesus, Thou Joy of Loving Hearts" (1858)

At the request of Professors Edward A. Park and Austin Phelps of Andover Seminary, the Rev. Ray Palmer contributed a number of hymns to the *Sabbath Hymn-Book.* Among his contributions were translations from the Latin, including "Jesus, Thou Joy of Loving Hearts"; attributed to Bernard of Clairvaux and written about A.D. 1140.

Many translations of the Latin hymn, which originally contained fifty four-line stanzas, have been produced. The best and most used of the German versions is that of Count Nicholas von Zinzendorf. Palmer's free paraphrase of Bernard's hymn is one of countless English translations; but, of all the versions produced to date, it is by far the most popular.[2] His translation uses stanzas 4, 3, 16, 24, and 10- in that order.[3] Albert Edward Bailey, in *The Gospel in Hymns,* notes that "in translating the Latin Dr. Palmer did not take the stanzas consecutively, but picked out certain ones that especially met his own spirit, then he paraphrased rather than translated, free to give his own slant to the thought in his own imagery."[4]

Ray Palmer was born on November 12, 1808, at Little Compton, Rhode Island, the son of a judge. His youth was spent in Boston where he was a clerk in a dry-goods store and a very active member of the Park Street Congregational Church. The Rev. Sereno Dwight was the pastor, and under his influence, Palmer decided to enter the ministry. After spending three years in preparatory work at Phillips Academy in Andover, he went to Yale University, where he graduated in 1830. For five years after his graduation he studied theology and taught at a New York girls' school. Ray Palmer was ordained in 1835 and spent the next thirty years equally divided between the Central Congregational Church in Bath, Maine, and the First Congregational Church in Albany, New York. In 1865 he was appointed the corresponding secretary of the American Congregational Union, a job from which he retired in 1878. Upon retirement he moved to Newark, New Jersey, where he died on March 29, 1887.

Works by Ray Palmer include: *Memoirs and Select Remains of Charles Pond*, 1829; *Doctrinal Textbook*, 1839; *Spiritual Improvement*, 1839; *Remember Me* or *The Holy Communion*, 1865; *Hymns and Sacred Pieces, with Miscellaneous Poems*, 1865; *Hymns of My Holy Hours and Other Pieces*, 1868; and *Voices of Hope and Gladness*, 1891.

Dr. Julian commented that Palmer's hymns, "by their combination of thought, poetry, and devotion, are superior to almost all others of American origin." Palmer never permitted anyone to revise his texts and refused to take any payment for his hymns.[5]

NOTES

1. Armin Haeussler, *The Story of Our Hymns*, Eden Publishing House, St. Louis, Missouri, 1952, p. 837.

2. Ibid., pp. 370–371.

3. *Handbook of the Hymnal*, edited by William Chalmers Covert and Calvin Weiss Lauffer, Presbyterian Board of Christian Education, Philadelphia, 1936, p. 375.

4. Albert Edward Bailey, *The Gospel in Hymns*, Charles Scribner's Sons, New York, 1950, p. 255.

5. Haeussler, *op. cit.*, p. 837.

The 100th Anniversary of The Creed of 1883
(1883)

This creed was published on December 19, 1883, bearing the approving signatures of twenty-two of the twenty-five men who had been commissioned to prepare it. Two refused to have their names attached because the new creed did not express their views adequately.[1] They were conservatives—representative of a portion of Congregational churches that rejected the confession because it lacked the kind of traditional statements on predestination that were so characteristic of the Westminster and Savoy documents.[2] The third man's name was not attached because he was absent from the meetings of the commission.[3]

The Congregationalists now had the kind of confession that no other major denomination in America could claim to have: "a widely recognized creed, of modern composition, and expressing a fair consensus of the present belief of the communion whose faith it set forth," and not binding on the churches any further than they chose to adopt it as a local expression of faith.[4]

The need for such a creed was voiced when the Congregationalist Association met in Wellington, Ohio, 1879, and called upon the National Council of the Congregational Churches in the United States to prepare "a formula that shall not be mainly a reaffirmation of the former confessions, but that shall state in precise terms in our living tongue the doctrines we hold today."[5] This matter was laid before the National Council the following year, along with similar requests from the General Conference of Minnesota and a Conference in Tennessee.[6]

Though it had been adopted enthusiastically by the Congregational Churches on June 23, 1865, the limitations of the Burial Hill Declaration had soon become apparent. As the years passed it became increasingly evident that a new confession of faith was desireable.[7] The Burial Hill Declaration was judged to be too rhetorical in form, too indefinite in statement with regard to particular doctrines, and too sweeping in its approval of seventeenth-century formulations of belief to be satisfactory as a creed for local churches. Nor was it an adequate exposition of the faith of the Congregational body as a whole.[8] New churches were springing into being—especially in the West—and there was a growing demand for a brief and modern confession of faith.[9] This desire had been expressed at National Council in 1871 but it was the request of the Ohio Association nearly a decade later that provided the impulse needed to get the work of preparation started.

The Council responded to the Association's request by appointing a Committee of Seven on November 15, 1880, to select twenty-five commissioners, representing different shades of thought and widely distributed geographically, to prepare a new creed. The members of the commission were free to adopt their own methods of procedure, but the Council imposed one stipulation— "that the result of their labors, when complete be reported—not to this Council, but to the churches and to the world through the public press—to carry such weight of authority as the character of the Commission and the intrinsic merit of their exposition of truth may command."[10] The chairman of the commission was the Rev. Julius II. Seelye, president of Amherst College.

J. L. Neve, in *Churches and Sects of Christendom*, wrote concerning the Creed of 1883 that this was

> the first real attempt at an independent American Confession for the Congregational Churches. . . . It was a Confession with a decidely evangelical ring . . . but this Confession never became more than an unadopted report of a commission appointed under the direction of the National Council of the Congregational Churches. . . . The fact that it served as the basis for many local Confessions and was immediately adopted by hundreds of churches showed that the Congregationalists were yet far from marching in the direction of the Unitarians.[12]

NOTES

1. Williston Walker, *A History Of The Congregationalist Churches In The United States*, The American Church History Series, 1894, p. 414.

2. J. L. Neve, *Churches and Sects of Christendom*, Lutheran Publishing House, Blair, Nebraska, Rev. Ed. 1944, p. 408.

3. Walker, *op. cit.*, p. 414.

4. Ibid.

5. Neve, *op. cit.*, p. 407.

6. Walker, *op. cit.*, p. 413.

7. Neve, *op. cit.*, p. 407.

8. Walker, *op. cit.*, p. 413.

9. Neve, *op. cit.*, p. 407.

10. Walker, *op. cit.*, p. 413.

11. Albert E. Dunning, *Congregationalists in America*, J.A. Hill & Co., New York, 1894, p. 529.

12. Neve, *op. cit.*, pp. 407–408. The text of the Creed of 1883 can be seen in Albert E. Dunning's *Congregationalists in America, op. cit.*, pp. 529–531, and in *History of American Congregationalism*, by Gaius Glenn Atkins and Frederick L. Fagley, The Pilgrim Press, Boston, 1942, pp. 402–404.

The 75th Anniversary of John Oxenham's Hymn, "In Christ There Is No East or West" (1908)

At the request of his nephew, the Rev. Dugald Macfayden, William Dunkerley, writing under the pen name "John Oxenham", wrote the entire script and planned all the scenes for the *Pageant of Darkness and Light*, including the words of "In Christ There Is No East or West".

A month-long exhibition and celebration of Christian missions, called "The Orient in London", sponsored by the London Missionary Society, was held in the Agricultural Hall, Islington, London, in 1908. A pageant depicting the triumphs of the Christian missionary cause was to be presented and the Rev. Macfayden was put in charge of producing it.[1] The work of William Dunkerley, Macfayden's uncle, met with great success. Between 1908 and 1914, the *Pageant* was widely performed throughout England and America. Besides the hymn, it contained such parts as the Livingstone Lament, the Hindoo Prayers, and the Hawaiian rhythmic strains, ending with the Procession of Nations:

> Through tribulations and distress,
> They come!
> Through perils great and bitterness,
> Through persecutions pitiless,
> They come!
> They come by paths the martyrs trod,
> They come from underneath the rod,
> Climbing through the darkness up to God,
> They come!
> Out of mighty tribulation,
> With a sound of jubilation,
> They come, they come.[2]

One newspaper, commenting on the initial exhibition, wrote that

> One got a vivid conception of the heroic stuff mis-
> sionaries are made of when they were seen penetrating
> the frozen lands of the north and the undertrodden depths
> of darkest Africa. It was easier to realize what Mr. Win-
> ston Churchill meant in his speech, when he opened the
> Exhibition, when he spoke of the civilizing and human-
> itarian work of the missionaries, which has for its motive
> force their zeal to win the savage and superstitious hearts
> of the heathen to the rule of Christ.[3]

Undoubtedly the most enduring part of the *Pageant* is the hymn, "In Christ There is No East or West". It brings to mind the words of the Apostle Paul in Gala-tians 3:23, and has been compared with the following poem by Rudyard Kipling:

> Oh, East is East, and West is West, and never the
>   twain shall meet,
> Till Earth and Sky stand presently at God's great Judg-
>   ment Seat.
> But there is neither East nor West, Border, nor Breed,
>   nor Birth,
> When two strong men stand face to face, though they
>   come from the ends of the earth."

It is noted that Kipling's poem is occupied with rigid racial barriers. Oxenham's hymn "while not ignoring these, takes account of the irresistible spirit of broth-erhood which is released by the gospel of Christ, a spirit which will eventually break down every barrier. God does not love walls. Christ came to demolish them."[4]

The hymn first appeared in Dunkerley's first book of

verses, *Bees in Amber,* in 1913. Since he was known only as a novelist, the publishers insisted on an edition of only two hundred copies. They soon realized their mistake, and by 1942, 286,000 copies had been issued.[5]

William Arthur Dunkerley was born on November 12, 1852, at Manchester, England. His father, who was a wholesale provision merchant, served for thirty years as superintendent of the Sunday School and for some time as deacon and treasurer of Charlton Road Church, Manchester. William's Sunday School teacher, James Windsor, gave each of his pupils a copy of Charles Kingsley's book *Westward Ho!,* when they reached a certain age. One of the main characters in Kingsley's book was John Oxenham—the name that young Dunkerley later adopted as his nom de plume.

Following his graduation from Victoria University in Manchester, William Dunkerley took charge of the French branch of his father's business and lived in Rennes, Brittany. Shortly after his marriage in 1877, he went with his bride to New York intending to establish a branch provision house in the United States. While living in Orange, New Jersey, he and his wife joined the Congregational Church in the community. When business failed, he traveled in Georgia and Florida, exploring the possibility of growing oranges and raising sheep. Dunkerley became interested in publishing and was especially attracted by the style of writing that appeared in the *Detroit Free Press.*

He returned to England and with an American, Robert Barr, established a London Branch of the *Detroit Free Press.* This lasted from 1882 to 1890. After helping to publish *The Idler* and *Today*—both of which were short lived—his career as a publisher ended in 1897.[6]

Writing as a diversion, Dunkerley published more than

forty novels in rapid succession, as well as twenty other volumes of prose and poetry. A deeply religious trend runs through a majority of his works—especially those written after 1921.[7] The British "Who's Who" states that he took up writing "as an alleviative and alternative from business and found it much more enjoyable, so dropped business and stuck to writing."[8]

To keep the identity of "John Oxenham" secret, William Dunkerley had all his correspondence handled by an agent. The secret was so strictly kept that for many years even some of his most intimate friends did not know who this mysterious "John Oxenham" was. Toward the end of his life he was simply known as "J.O." by his friends and nearest associates. He died on January 24, 1941.[9]

Once Dunkerley received a letter containing these words:

> This is being written on board R.M.S. . . . somewhere in the Pacific. I feel you may like to hear about a rather unique service on board today. It was led by a Swede, a Brigadier in the Salvation Army, who spoke of his work in famine relief in China, among lepers in the East Indies, and head-hunters and cannibals in the Celebes. His audience consisted of British, Americans, Chinese, two Germans and one Italian. We began and ended the meeting by singing "In Christ There is No East or West". A meeting like this fills me with hope for the future.[10]

NOTES

1. Armin Haeussler, *The Story of Our Hymns,* Eden Publishing House, St. Louis, Missouri, 1952, p. 421; Albert C. Ronander and Ethel K. Porter, *Guide To the Pilgrim Hymnal,* United Church Press, 1966, p. 319.

2. H. Augustine Smith, Lyric Religion: *The Romance of Immortal Hymns,* D. Appelton-Century Company, New York and London, 1931, p. 171.

3. Haeussler, *op. cit.*, p. 421.

4. *Handbook To The Hymnal*, edited by William Chalmers Covert and Calvin Weiss Lauffer, Presbyterian Board of Christian Education, Philadelphia, 1936, p. 362; Ronander and Porter, *op. cit.*, p. 319.

5. *The Hymnal 1940 Companion*, the Protestant Episcopal Church, The Church Pension Fund, New York, 1951, p. 174.

6. An extensive and interesting biography can be found in Armin Haeussler's *The Story of Our Hymns, op. cit.*, pp. 833–834.

7. *Hymnal 1940 Companion, op. cit.*, p. 524.

8. H. Augustine Smith, *op. cit.*, p. 170.

9. Haeussler, *op. cit.*, p. 834.

10. *Hymnal 1940 Companion, op. cit.*, p. 174.

The 50th Anniversary of Henry Hallam Tweedy's Hymn, "O Spirit of the Living God" (1933)

In a letter to Dr. Robert Guy McCutchan, Henry Tweedy wrote concerning this hymn:

> "O Spirit of the Living God" was written just before the churches proposed to celebrate the supposed anniversary of Pentecost. Some of the Old Pentecostal hymns were to me unsatisfactory, and I was eager to interpret the symbolism of the story in Acts in a way that modern man could understand and sincerely mean. Unless I am mistaken, the Methodist hymnal is the first to use this. My memory is that my colleague, Professor Halford E. Luccock, asked for it and sent it to the committee."[1]

Henry Hallam Tweedy was born of Scottish ancestry on August 5, 1868, in Binghamton, New York. He went to Yale in 1901. He prepared for the ministry at Union Theological Seminary in New York City, and the University of Berlin. He was granted his M.A. degree from Yale in 1909.

After being ordained into the Congregational ministry in 1898, Henry Tweedy served as the pastor of the Plymouth Church in Utica, New York, until 1902, and as pastor of South Church, Bridgeport, Connecticut, from 1902 to 1909. For the next twenty-eight years of his life, he was Professor of Practical Theology at Yale Divinity School.[2] Despite a Vandyke beard and a somewhat formal manner, it is reported that he was very popular with preparatory school boys and college students.[3]

Tweedy is the author of a number of books including, *The Ministry and The War*, 1918; *The Christian Ministry*, 1922; and *The Minister and His Hymnal*. With Dr. Luther A. Weigle, he was the joint editor and author of *King's Highway Series of Ethical and Religious Readers, Religious Training in the School and Home,* and *Training the Devotional Life*. In 1939 he compiled the hymnal *Christian Worship and Praise*.[4]

In 1928 Henry Tweedy received first prize from the Hymn Society of America for a hymn, "Eternal God, Whose Power Hold", which was selected from more than a thousand submitted. Dedicated to maintaining a high standard in hymnwriting, Henry Hallam Tweedy exerted a great influence upon 20th century American hymnody.[5] He died on September 11, 1953.

NOTES

1. Armin Haeussler, *The Story of Our Hymns*, Eden Publishing House, St. Louis, Missouri, 1952, p. 241.

2. Ibid., p. 949.

3. Albert C. Ronander and Ethel K. Porter, *Guide To The Pilgrim Hymnal*, United Church Press, 1966, p. 235.

4. Haussler, *op. cit.*, p. 949.

5. Ronander and Porter, *op. cit.*, pp. 234–235.

The 25th Anniversary of The Death of Harry Thomas Stock, Expert in Youth Ministry (1958)

It was said of Dr. Harry Stock that "few churchmen during the first half of the twentieth century devoted themselves with greater dedication and effectiveness to the religious training of American young people."[1] He served as the secretary of the Department of Student Life and Young Peoples Work of the Congregational Education Society from 1922 to 1938. After 1938 he served as General Secretary of the Division of Christian Education of the Board of Home Missions of the Congregational Christian Churches. Besides making numerous contributions to magazines, Harry Thomas Stock produced several books, including: *Church Work With Young People*, 1927; *Christian Life Problems*, 1927; *Problems of Christian Youth*, 1928; *So This is Missions*, 1933; *Better Meetings For The Young Peoples Society*, 1933; *A Life and A Living*, 1936; and *Preparing For a Life Work*, 1936.[2]

Stock's hymn, *O Gracious God, Whose Constant Care*, first published in *The Congregationalist* February 12, 1931, was written for a vesper service at a summer youth conference. With one stanza deleted, it was included in *The Hymnal*, published in 1941: "Vesper hour" was changed to "sacred hour" in the third stanza to make the hymn suitable for general use.[3]

Harry Thomas Stock was born on November 10, 1891, at Springfield, Illinois. He graduated from Knox College in 1914 and from Chicago Theological Seminary in 1916. The following year he earned his M.A. degree at the University of Chicago and became the associate professor in Church History at Chicago Theological Seminary—a position he held for five years.[4] In 1922, Stock became a denominational director of work with young people in churches—a field in which he became a widely-recognized authority. Later, in the 1940s, he became General Secretary of the Division of Christian Education, Board of Home Missions, of the Congregational Christian Churches. He held this position until his death.

NOTES

1. *Guide To The Pilgrim Hymnal,* Albert C. Ronander and Ethel K. Porter, United Church Press, Philadelphia and Boston, 1966, p. 370.
2. Armin Haeussler, *The Story of Our Hymns,* Eden Publishing Houses, St. Louis, Missouri, 1952, p. 923.
3. *Guide To The Pilgrim Hymnal, op. cit.,* p. 371.
4. *The Story Of Our Hymns, op. cit.,* p. 923.

Anniversaries of the Christian Stream

The 175th Anniversary of The Beginning of Elias Smith's Publishing of The Herald of Gospel Liberty (1808)

On September 1, the first issue of the first religious newspaper in the world came off the press in Portsmouth, New Hampshire. The title was chosen carefully, and year after year the publication lived up to its title. In 1805 the Rev. Elias Smith had published a quarterly, *The Christian's Magazine*. In it he treated various religious subjects. Several other similar publications existed; but Smith's publication in 1808 fit into a category different from anything the world had ever seen before. Following are some quotations from that first issue.

> Address to the public. To the subscribers for this paper, and to all who may hereafter read its contents—
> Brethren and Fellow-Citizens: The age in which we live may certainly be distinguished from others in the history of man, and particularly as it respects the people of these United States; the increase of knowledge is very great in different parts of the world, and of course there is an increase of Liberty among the people, and an increasing desire among certain individuals, accompanied with their fruitless exertions, to prevent them from enjoying what they have been taught belongs to them, as a right given by their Creator, and guaranteed by the government of the country in which they live. . . .

141

A member of Congress said to me not long ago (while speaking upon the state of the people in this country, as it respects religious liberty) to this amount: 'The people in this country are in general free, as to political matters; but in the things of religion, multitudes of them are apparently ignorant of what liberty is.' This is true. Many who appear to know what belongs to them as citizens, and who will contend for their rights, when they talk or act upon things of the highest importance, appear to be guided wholly by the opinions of designing men, who would bind them in the chains of ignorance all their days and entail the same on all their posterity. The design of this paper is to show the liberty which belongs to men, as it respects their duty to God, and each other. . . .

A religious newspaper is almost a new thing under the sun. I know not but this is the first ever published to the world.

The Utility of such a paper has been suggested to me, from the great use other papers are to the community at large. In this way almost the whole state of the world is presented to us at once. . . . If we are profited in political affairs in this way, I do not see why the knowledge of the Redeemer's kingdom may not be promoted or increased in the same way. It appears to me best to make the trial . . .

It may be that some may wish to know why this paper should be named 'The Herald of Gospel Liberty'. This kind of liberty is the only one which can make us happy, being the glorious liberty of the sons of God which Christ proclaimed, and which is given and enjoined by the law of liberty; which is the law of the spirit of life in Christ Jesus, which makes free from the law of sin and death.[1]

The Rev. Elias Smith, a Baptist minister, joined Abner Jones, who, in opposition to Calvinist Baptist views,

142

organized the First Free Christian Church at Lyndon, Vermont, in 1801. Jones insisted that Christian character should be the only requirement for church membership and rejected the practice of closed communion. The churches following the principles of Jones and Smith, and known as the "Christian Connection", met in their first General Christian Conference at Windham, Conn. in 1820.

An earlier group who called themselves "Christian", was founded by James O'Kelley in 1794. O'Kelley's followers were known as the "Republican Methodists", but eventually the name "The Christian Church" was adopted. These "Christians" declared that the Bible would be their only guide.

A later group to call themselves "Christian" was founded by Barton Stone, whose opposition to Calvinist theology led him to withdraw from the Presbyterian Synod of Kentucky in 1803. Many of his eight thousand followers united with those of Thomas and Alexander Campbell to form the Disciples of Christ at Lexington, Kentucky, in 1832. Those who did not unite with the Disciples ultimately joined the O'Kelley and Jones-Smith Christians and became part of the Christian Connection or Conference.[2]

Elias Smith's *The Herald of Gospel Liberty* not only provided a means of dispensing religious knowledge; it was also a channel for co-ordination and mutual understanding in the Christian Church, early becoming that denomination's official organ. In his book *The Christian Denomination and Christian Doctrine,* Simon Addison Bennett writes that "it was through correspondence, itinerant ministers, and *The Herald of Gospel Liberty* that the three groups of Christians became acquainted, found they were on the same platform and recognized each

143

other. This publication had more to do with this than any other agency."[3]

Through letters to the editor from readers of the earliest issues of *The Herald of Gospel Liberty*, the Rev. Elias Smith learned of the existence of the southern Christians. William Lanpier, of Alexandria, Virginia, wrote to Smith inquiring about the "name, discipline, form of Church government, doctrine, and extent" of the New England group. Late in 1808, the editor received a letter from Robert Punshon that stated:

> In Virginia about 16 years ago it pleased the Lord to call out from the body of Methodists, Baptists, and Presbyterians a people into Gospel order, laying the foundation on Moses and the Prophets, Jesus Christ being the chief corner stone. . . . The Church has spread through Virginia, North and South Carolina, Georgia, Tennessee, Kentucky, Ohio, and the Western part of the state of Pennsylvania, where there are thousands united in the same spirit worshipping the Lord.[4]

At about the same time, Smith received a letter from Elder Jonathan Foster of Winchester, Virginia, who informed the editor of his intention to publish a pamphlet entitled, "A Scriptural Description of a True Christian Church." He concluded his letter with the words, "My Brother, we have no reverend, nor right reverends among us, no masters—we are all brethren."

Several months later, a letter was received from William Guirey describing the southern Church:

> After we became a separate people, three points were determined on, 1st. No head over the church but Christ. 2nd. No confession of faith, articles of religion, rubic canons, creeds, etc. but the New Testament. 3rd. No religious name but christians. For several years I have

144

been a minister in this church and have traveled among the members from Philadelphia to the Southern frontier of Georgia. We have members in every state south of the Potomac, also a few churches in Pennsylvania; from the best information I can obtain I suppose there are about 20,000 people in the Southern and Western States who call themselves by the *christian name*.[5]

NOTES

1. Simon Addison Bennett, *The Christian Denomination and Christian Doctrine*, The Christian Publishing Association, Dayton, Ohio, pp. 25–26.

2. *History and Program of the United Church of Christ*, United Church Press, 1978, pp. 15–16.

3. Bennett, pp. 26–27.

4. *A History Of The Christian Church In The South*, Durward T. Stokes and William T. Scott, Elon College, 1973, pp. 38–39.

5. Ibid.

The 125th Anniversary of The Rev. Thomas Bashaw's Attempt to Get Christians to Define Their Doctrinal Position (1858)

The two-year old Southern Christian Convention was holding its first regular meeting at Cypress Chapel, Nansemond County, Virginia, from May 5 to May 8, 1858. Warned in advance that there would be strong opposition to his proposal and knowing that it would cause a great stir of excitement, the Rev. Thomas Bashaw, the young and eager pastor of the Christian Church at New Bern, North Carolina, arose to his feet and read a resolution: "*Resolved*, that this Convention take into consideration the expediency or inexpediency of defining our position as a denomination upon the leading doctrines of the Holy Scriptures, which we claim as the foundation and creed of our church."

This was the climax of an effort that had occupied a major part of Bashaw's attention through the spring of 1858. This delegate from the Eastern Virginia Conference was convinced that those who had met at Union Chapel, Alamance County, North Carolina, in the fall of 1856, and brought the Southern Christian Convention into being, had not gone far enough in establishing a doctrinal position for the denomination; and that, as a result, this new denomination was greatly misunderstood by others who knew nothing of its teachings.

Besides supporting a strong statement opposing the abolitionist sentiments of their northern Christian brethren, the delegates to the 1856 Convention adopted the following fundamentals of the Christian Church:

1. Christ the only head of the Church.

2. The name Christian to the exclusion of all party and sectarian names.

3. The Holy Bible or the Scriptures of the Old and New Testaments our only creed or confession of faith.

4. Christian character or vital piety the true scriptural test of fellowship and church membership.

5. The right of private judgment and the liberty of conscience the privilege and duty of all.

When the Convention ended, though a new denomination was born, many of the usual components of a denomination were lacking. For one thing, the Convention had no power to license, ordain, or station ministers. This and other major governing responsibilities still belonged to the various conferences. The Convention's role was apparently that of consultant, and its chief function was the sponsorship of several undertakings in education, publication, and mission. As time went on, the structural weaknesses became more and more apparent.

146

A decade later, the Rev. Solomon Apple—a delegate to that initial Convention—confessed in an address that "they adopted a manifesto, setting forth one reason for separation from the north, but the great principle which underlay the surface was entirely ignored." He went on to say that "two or three brief reports were made on the subject of church government. They put forth no religious directory, form of judicatory, or ceremonies for the celebration of matrimony, funeral rites, ordination of Elders and Deacons, or for the sacraments of baptism and the Lord's Supper."

In the spring of 1858, convinced that the organization of the new denomination was embarassingly incomplete, Thomas Bashaw sent a series of articles to the *Christian Sun*, describing in detail the improvements in church polity and practice that he deemed essential. Some of his suggestions brought forth only mild criticism, but one brought forth fiery opposition. In the March 5th issue of the *Sun* appeared these words:

> And see also, if something is not lacking, to secure us as a denomination, from the misrepresentation, which has been hurled from time to time against the Christians, and will continue to be hurled against them, until they take steps to put a stop to it, by presenting themselves in their true light, or true position before other denominations and the world at large, in reference to the faith and doctrines believed and held by them as a denomination. This the Christian church has never yet done, and this is one of the main things lacking now.

In their worship and in other aspects of their congregational life, the Christians closely resembled other Protestants, and for many this was not a cause of great concern. According to Thomas Bashaw, however, the new denomination was facing an identity crisis. There had been three distinct groups in the United States known as Christians. Each had evolved separately in a different part of the nation and initially had no formal contact with each other. They differed somewhat in their views, but all three had been falsely accused by other sects and denominations of heterodox beliefs. As the time approached for the holding of the first regular meeting of the Southern Christian Convention, Bashaw was suggesting that steps should be taken to solve this identity problem. The five principles adopted at the Convention in 1956 might have been sufficient for some, but Thomas Bashaw wanted the denomination's positions on doctrine and polity more clearly spelled out.

To promote action on this matter, he sent a proposal containing 28 Articles to the *Sun,* to be published before the next meeting of the Convention. The *Sun's* editor, The Rev. W. B. Wellons, published Bashaw's communication, but explained that the Articles would have to be omitted because they would require more than a page in the journal. He promised instead that the proposal would be presented at the Convention. On April 23, in explaining the omission of the Articles, the editor expressed his own personal view that "to adopt articles of faith as a denominational standard would be to adopt a creed." A week later Thomas Bashaw's reply appeared in the journal; "I have, and do still maintain that a declaration of Christian faith touching the principle doctrines of the Bible, is no human creed, no more a human creed, than the Bible itself, if that declaration is in accordance with, and sustainable by the plain teachings of the Holy Scriptures."

In support of the resolution that he presented to the Convention in May, Bashaw argued:

> We as a denomination ought to define what we are, and show the world what are our fundamental doc-

trines. . . . May I ask, what is the cause that the Church has not advanced? Why have we not a church in every village? The cause is we have not declared what we believe and have therefore suffered much slander.

Wellons took the lead in opposing the proposal and insisted that the Christian principles agreed upon at the prior Convention were adequate; adding that a further declaration of faith would be an "abridgment" and "mutilation" of the Word of God. The Convention rallied to Wellon's support and Bashaw's proposal was defeated.[1]

Thomas Bashaw had become acquainted with the Christian Church in 1853, when the Rev. M. B. Barrett organized a congregation in Wilmington, North Carolina. He became a member of that congregation the following year. He was ordained at Union, Southampton County, Virginia, in 1855, and was appointed to itinerant work. In 1857, he was appointed to preach for the congregations at New Bern and Goose Creek. It was while serving in that pastorate that he made his contributions to the *Sun* and suffered his defeat at the Convention.[2]

Within a decade, Thomas Bashaw had quietly dropped out of the Christian Church. However, the reasons he presented for clarifying the position of the southern Christians were recognized later as being sound. Ironically, it was the Rev. W. B. Wellons, who, two years later, felt compelled to publish a book in which he indignantly denied the charges made by the Rev. John Paris that Christians in the south had forsaken James O'Kelley's principles and had embraced Unitarianism. Several other such situations arose from time to time. Ten years later the decision of the Convention in 1858 was completely reversed, and Thomas Bashaw's efforts were vindicated.[3]

149

NOTES

1. *A History Of The Christian Church In The South,* Durward T. Stokes and William T. Scott, Elon College, 1973, pp. 85–89.
2. P. J. Kernodle, *Lives of Christian Ministers,* The Central Publishing Company, Richmond, Va., 1909.
3. *A History Of The Christian Church In The South, op. cit.,* p. 89.

The 100th Anniversary of The Founding of the Franklinton Literary and Theological Christian Institute (1883)

The efforts of the Rev. George Washington Dunn had not been in vain. He had succeeded in obtaining wide financial support for the higher education of Black southern Christians, and the circumstances were now favorable for the founding of the Institute at Franklinton. In support of that North Carolina school for Blacks, the North Carolina and Virginia Conference passed the following resolution in 1883:

> WHEREAS, We believe that this institution is doing a good work, in our midst, therefore, be it
> *Resolved,* That we bid Brother Young and those who have inaugurated this enterprise, God speed in their good work.
> *Resolved,* That we will co-operate with our brother in the education of our colored friends.

Shortly after the close of the Civil War, the Rev. George Washington Dunn, pastor of the Black Christian Church at Franklinton, became actively involved in an effort to provide educational opportunities for his people. As a result of the prodding by Dunn and by Sanford

L. Long, who was eager to provide greater educational advantages for his six children, the North Carolina Colored Conference voted in 1871 to establish a high school at Franklinton. A committee was appointed to purchase a lot, and there was much enthusiasm for the project. Sufficient funds were not available, however, and no immediate action was taken.

Sanford Long managed to provide such advantages for his six children "that his became one of the best educated Negro families in the state." In 1878, one of his sons, Henry Edward Long, started a private school in the Franklinton Christian Church, charging a tuition of twenty-five cents per pupil. The school was so well attended that it was necessary to employ an assistant for the second year, but this failed to meet the need for a high school. Recovery from post-war impoverishment in the South was so slow that it was difficult for the people of the South to provide the money needed for the education of either whites or Blacks.

If higher education was to become a reality for Black southern Christians, George W. Dunn realized that the appeal for financial assistance must reach into the northern states. Inspired by what he read in a copy of *The Golden Censer* [*Censor*], Dunn wrote an impassioned plea to its editor, telling him of the needs of his people.

Dunn's letter in *The Golden Censer* was read by William O. Cushing, a Christian minister in New York State, and forwarded to the *Herald of Gospel Liberty*, in which it appeared on February 31, 1880. In his letter, George W. Dunn explained that he had formerly been a slave, "but now, thank God, we are sitting under our own vine and fig tree, and can worship God according to our conscience." He wrote that he had been trying to preach for five years and belonged to the Christian Church. He then went on to decry the plight of Black Christians:

> The Baptist people, white teachers came from the North, and have built up schools for the colored Baptists. The Methodist white people have come from the North and built up schools for the Methodists, and are teaching the colored people. So with other sects. Therefore they are ahead of us in education. There is not one neither North nor South has ever come to relieve us of this state of poverty and ignorance. Our inducements are by other denominations saying, come and join us and deny your name and take ours and we will educate you. We sometimes are almost about to cry out like the trembling jailor and say what we must do to be saved. And again the Spirit of the Lord speaks like thunder, and tells us to stand still and see the salvation of God.

Dunn's letter concluded with a plea for assistance to the school at Franklinton, insisting that with such aid the Black Christians could soon begin to improve and help themselves.

George W. Dunn then wrote a letter to Editor T. M. McWhinney, in March 1880, thanking him for publishing his first letter in the *Herald* and for informing the North that a Black Christian denomination existed in the south. In the same letter, he noted that Black Christians could not supply their congregations with sufficient hymn books. As a result of this second letter, Dunn received hymnals and periodicals, including a box of twenty-five from Canada. These were immediately distributed and put to use.

Dunn's letters were read with sympathetic interest by J. P. Watson, Secretary of Missions in the northern church, and action was taken. In October, 1880, the Mission Board of the American Christian Convention sent George

Young, a minister of the New York Conference, to become the principal of the Franklinton school, with Henry Edward Long serving as his assistant. Jonathan E. Brush of New York published his appraisal of the beginning of Young's work at Franklinton, reporting that the white citizens of the town distrusted Young's mission. An arousing presidential campaign was being carried on throughout the nation, and people "conceived the idea that he came among them more for political than philanthropic motives." Young also learned that money was needed if the work he had undertaken was to be successful. "His students needed Bibles and textbooks. His ninety-five children were in a dilapidated building. They needed a schoolhouse and books suitable for instruction."

Brush visited Franklinton on January 11, 1881, at the request of J. P. Watson, who wanted a full report on the school for a presentation to the Christian Mission Board. The result was a successful drive for funds, which received such a favorable response from both whites and Blacks that a new school building was erected in 1882, and classes were no longer held in the church. The construction was supervised by J. W. Wellons, who convinced the neighbors that Young's work was commendable and worthy of their encouragement. Then, in 1883, came a resolution from the North Carolina and Virginia Conference supporting the work at Franklinton and the incorporation of the school.[1]

NOTE

1. Stokes, Durward T., and Scott, William T., *A History Of The Christian Church In The South*, Elon College, 1973, pp. 137–139.

The 100th Anniversary of The Beginnings of Foreign Mission Work in the Christian Church in the South (1883)

Responding to the persistent pleading of the Rev. Peter Thomas Klapp, the North Carolina and Virginia Conference at its 1883 session appointed a committee to study the subject of Foreign Missions. The six-member committee, headed by P. T. Klapp, made the following proposal to the Conference:

> WHEREAS, the cause of Foreign Missions is a work of such great magnitude that it demands the co-operation of the various branches of the Christian Church; therefore we recommend the following resolutions:
>
> 1. That our ministers be authorized to raise funds for Foreign Missions in or before the month of April and pay the same to the Treasurer of Conference to be used for the above purpose; and that a continued effort be made by us as a conference and people to raise funds for the aforesaid object.
>
> 2. That a committee on Foreign Missions by appointed by this Conference, and that this committee be authorized to correspond with the Secretary of Missions in the Christian Church North with the view of uniting our efforts and sending out one or two missionaries as soon as possible.

The report was adopted and a Conference Committee was appointed. According to the records, this was the first organized effort in the cause of foreign missions by the Southern Christian Church.

Several months before the North Carolina and Virginia Conference held its 1883 meeting in Moore County, North Carolina, P. T. Klapp had an interesting experience in Moore Union Church. Concluding his sermon on the condition of "the Cannibals," he was confronted by a man named R. Womack who said to him, "if your statement is true, I must help. I have but 35 cents—take it and use it to aid in sending the gospel to that benighted people." Challenged by that meeting with Womack, Peter Thomas Klapp made the work of Foreign Missions a primary concern for a number of years. To him belonged the "proud distinction of being the father of the Foreign Mission work in the Christian Church."[1]

NOTE

1. Stokes, Durwart T., and Scott, William T. *A History Of The Christian Church In The South*, Elon College, 1973, pp. 194, 195.

SUGGESTIONS
FOR OBSERVING THESE
ANNIVERSARIES IN
1983 AND BEYOND

1. Celebrate the 500th Anniversary of Martin Luther's birthday with Lutherans.

In spite of the differing views of Luther and Ulrich Zwingli concerning the Lord's Supper, Lutherans and the "Evangelical-Reformed" aspect of the United Church of Christ have held many doctrinal views in common, sharing a common Reformation heritage. Until recently, union churches have been a familiar form of church life in certain areas, with Lutherans and Reformed congregations sharing a single building. Quite often, Lutheran and Reformed church members have intermarried and worshiped with their families at each other's services on alternate Sundays. The number of Union churches has dwindled, and today members of the United Church of Christ and Lutheran Churches find fewer occasions to experience church fellowship together. Reformation Sunday or November 13—the Sunday nearest to Luther's birthday—would provide a good occasion to hold a joint service in observance of the 500th anniversary of Luther's birth in celebration of their common indebtedness to the man who started the Protestant Reformation.

Recall that it was on the occasion of the 300th anniversary of the beginning of the Reformation (1817) that the Evangelical Church of the Prussian Union was born. (See page 00.) Frederick William III of Prussia declared that this was an appropriate occasion to decree that Lutherans and Reformed no longer existed in his realm as separate denominations, but as Evangelicals. The Augsburg Confession and Luther's Small Catechism were a part of the creedal heritage of the German Evangelicals who settled in mid-western United States and who became the Evangelical Synod of North America.

Further note that Thomas Cramner and other leaders of the English Reformation had contacts with churches on the continent and were influenced by Luther's teachings. English refugees, fleeing the wrath of Bloody Mary, also came into contact with those teachings. Upon their return to England, they contributed to the general Protestant milieu out of which English Puritanism and Congregationalism sprang.

2. Use the year to reflect upon the role of Christian higher education and theological training in today's world.

Twelve of the 59 anniversaries celebrate the founding of Christian colleges or theological seminaries. This is a highly secular and technological age in which we live. How do church-sponsored institutions of higher education survive and continue to be faithful to their founding principles in such an age? How effective are they in making a Christian impact upon society?

The year 1983 would be a good year to invite professors and administrative leaders from United Church of

158

Christ colleges and seminaries to come to our congregations and discuss the issues currently confronting Christian Higher Education. We need not be limited to our denomination. If a college or seminary of another denomination is nearby, invite its professors or administrators to share their views on crises confronting their institutions with you.

Congregations that make special contributions in support of the particular colleges or seminaries mentioned on these pages, or graduates from such institutions, will, of course, want to pay special attention to the anniversary observances.

3. Conduct mini-courses for older youth and adults.
● Plan a series of biographical studies on "Famous Persons in U.C.C. History to Recall in 1983". The series could include: Zacharias Ursinus, Robert Browne, Roger Williams, Jonathan Edwards, and Sara Pierpont Edwards. An extended series might include: Hermann Garlichs, Friedrich Schmid, William Ames, John Owen, Nathaniel Taylor, Harry Thomas Stock, Elias Smith, Thomas Bashaw and George Washington Dunn.

Different members of the group may select one of the persons for doing research and for reporting to the group. Plan a study of the beginnings of Congregationalism. With so many noteworthy anniversaries clustered around the early years of the Congregationalists in England and America, such a study seems appropriate. Center your study around the life and work of Robert Browne and Roger Williams.
Plan a brief study of the beginnings of the Evangelical Synod of North America, noting the pioneering work of Hermann Garlichs and Friedrich Schmid.

Note: United Church of Christ anniversaries in 1984 will include the 500th anniversary of the birthday of

159

Ulrich Zwingli, the 475th anniversary of the birthday of John Calvin, the 275th anniversary of the flight from the Palatinate and the beginning of the German Reformed migration to America, the 100th anniversary of the death of Friedrich Ernst Daniel Schleiermacher, and the 200th anniversary of the Christmas Conference in Baltimore, which provoked James O'Kelley's departure from the Methodist Church. This suggests that studies of the study of the beginnings of the Reformed Church, the Evangelical Synod, and the Christian Churches might well be postponed until 1984.

• Plan a study of the role of creeds in the life and worship of one of the four streams that make up the United Church of Christ. For instance, study the creedal development in the Congregational Churches (Savoy Declaration, Saybrook Platform, Browne's Treatises, the Creed of 1883); the use of creedal statements to determine the eligibility to serve as seminary professors (Andover and Hartford); or the difficulty of Thomas Bashaw in persuading the Christian Church to put its doctrinal position into a written form.

Ingredients of the study may include: creedal statements in the Bible, the use of baptismal creeds in the early church as a test of faith, the development of the Apostles and Nicene Creeds; and the Heidelberg Catechism (the anniversary of Ursinus' death). The 25th anniversary of the Statement of Faith will be celebrated in 1984. You may want to postpone this study until next year.

• Plan a study of the doctrinal concepts of God and sin in today's world. The world is divided between persons who put their faith in the accomplishments of God, and those who put their faith in the achievements of man.

Persons with faith in God believe in an iminent, sovereign God who accomplishes the divine purposes through the Spirit's working in human lives and events. The universe for such persons is more or less God-centered. Sin—alienation from God and a thwarting of God's purposes—is a reality for them. For many others in our time who see only the amazing scientific, cultural and technological accomplishments of the human race and who put their faith solely in human capabilities, God and sin do not appear to be real at all.

There is currently a conservative trend manifested in all aspects of life, including religion. The New Evangelicalism, the Moral Majority, the creationist's attempt to have the biblical story of creation taught as science in the public school, the prospering of fundamentalistic churches—all are indicative of this trend. For persons in the conservative camp, God and sin are very real and feature largely in daily thought and conversation. For others, with a more decidedly humanistic bent; God, sin and the supernatural rarely enter into thought or conversation.

Your group, reflecting on the anniversary of Ursinus' death, may find it helpful to discuss the concepts of God and sin as set forth in the Heidelberg Catechism. You may want to observe the anniversary of the death of Jonathan Edwards and of the death of Nathaniel Taylor by studying the theological controversies that led to the founding of Andover and Hartford Seminaries. Edwards was a typical strict Calvinist, who maintained that all men were totally depraved and that the election of some to salvation and others to damnation was wholly the act of a sovereign God. Since God is infinitely good and wise, even the arbitrary damnation of sinners can be seen as serving God's ultimate purposes. Nathaniel Taylor, on the other hand, was a moderate Calvinist, who argued that sinners are punished because they have freely chosen evil. If the just and sovereign God punishes the sinner, this indicates that the sinner indeed has free will.

Your group may want to discuss the current views on predestination and free will. Note that the Creed of 1883 was the first Congregational creed to make no mention of predestination. Examine what the United Church Statement of Faith declares about God and sin. Find out what is currently being written about God and sin by leading theologians of our day.

You may want to note the nearly pantheistic views of God in Horace Bushnell's *Nature and the Supernatural* and his difficulty in maintaining the true humanity of Christ. You may want to reflect on contemporary groups or movements that may manifest similar views.

4. Plan a "World Ministries Exhibition"—your own "Pageant of Darkness and Light".

In observance of the 75th anniversary of John Oxenham's hymn "In Christ There is No East or West," your congregation or association may want to place special emphasis upon the work of the United Church Board For World Ministries. Let "In Christ There is No East or West" be your theme hymn and tell the story of how that hymn was written. Have booths or displays set up in various parts of the building depicting work being done through the World Board in various parts of the world today. Use pictures, tapes, brochures, maps, and missionaries on furlough to tell the story. Be prepared to show films and filmstrips on the work of the Board continuously in a darkened room.

Special attention in your exhibition could be called to the 100th anniversary of the Evangelical Synod's acceptance of a mission field in India, and to the 100th anniversary of the beginning of foreign mission work by the Christian Church in the South. Yours could be an exhibition that traces the history of the work of world missions in the four denominations that became the United Church of Christ. The hymn "In Christ There Is No East or West" could have special meaning for a World Communion Sunday Service. The story of the hymn could appear on an insert in the weekly bulletin for that Sunday.

5. Put on a hymn festival.

● Plan a "Hymns of the United Church of Christ Anniversary Hymn Festival". Your program will include the singing of one or two stanzas of the following:

—Julius H. Horstmann's translations: "God of Might, We Praise Thy Name", "The Work is Thine, O Christ Our Lord", and "Wait on God, and Trust Him".

—Ray Palmer's translation, "Jesus, Thou Joy of Loving Hearts".

—John Oxenham's hymn, "In Christ There Is No East or West".

—Henry Hallam Tweedy's hymn, "O Spirit of the Living God".

—Harry Thomas Stock's, "O Gracious God, Whose Constant Care."

Tell the stories of these hymns, hymnwriters, or hymn translators when you introduce each hymn. You may also include Henry Harbaugh's "Jesus, I Live To Thee"; sung to Isaac Baker Woodbury's tune, *Lake Enon.* Tell the story of the composer as well.

Since at least half of these hymns may be unfamiliar to the average congregation, they could be sung as anthems by the choir. A special attempt may be made to learn these hymns.

If no hymn festival is planned, these hymns could be

sung by congregations or choirs on Sundays throughout the year, with their stories told by the pastor. The stories might also be included in inserts in the weekly bulletins or in parish newsletters.

• Based on the 125th anniversary of Ray Palmer's translation, "Jesus, Thou Joy of Loving Hearts", and the 75th anniversary of Julius H. Horstmann's translations, plan a "Hymn Festival Honoring Hymn Translators." The year 1983 marks the 125th anniversary of hymn translations by Catherine Winkworth: "Blessed Jesus, at Thy Word", "Light of Light, Enlighten Me", "Now Thank We All Our God", "Arise, the Kingdom is at Hand", "Wake, Awake, for Night is Flying", and "All My Heart This Night Rejoices". It also marks the 125th anniversary of Jane Borthwick's "Allelulia, Fairest Morning", of Edward Caswall's "When Morning Gilds The Skies", and of Sarah Borthwick Findlater's "O Happy Home, Where Thou Art Loved the Dearest." A hymn festival limited to these hymn translations and the stories of the translators could be planned for a congregation, association or community, at any time during the year.

6. Dramatize one or more of the anniversaries.

There may be talented persons in congregations or associations who would be capable of writing and producing a play that depicts the life and works of such persons as Jonathan Edwards, Robert Browne, or Roger Williams. Producing a play can involve many persons in meaningful and self-rewarding ways. This could be a real challenge to persons who enjoy creative writing. Instead of a play, creative writers could be challenged to write and present monologues or choral readings depicting the lives and contributions of persons mentioned on these pages.

7. Use quotations from Jonathan Edwards.

The following quotations from the writings of Jonathan Edwards could be used in Sunday bulletins or parish newsletters anytime, but especially during 1983.

Affections
Although to true religion there must indeed be something else beside affections; yet true religion consists so much in the affections, that there can be no true religion without them. He who has no religious affection is in a state of spiritual death.

—*Religious Affections*, 1818

Beauty
We see the most proper image of the beauty of Christ when we see beauty in the human soul.

—*Representative Selections*

God's Wrath
The God that holds you over the pit of hell, much as one holds a spider, or some loathsome insect, over the fire, abhors you, and is dreadfully provoked: his wrath towards you burns like fire; he looks upon you as worthy of nothing else, but to be cast into the fire.

—*Sinners in the Hands of an Angry God*, 1741

God
God . . . stands in no need of, cannot be profited by, or receive anything from the creature, or be truly hurt, or be the subject of any suffering or impair of his glory and felicity from any other being.

—*On the End of Creation*, 1765

Kingdom of Heaven

A time of great light and knowledge . . . it [The Kingdom of Heaven on Earth]shall be a time of great holiness . . . it will be a time of excellent order in the church of Christ . . . ease, quietness, pleasantness, and cheerfulness of mind, also wealth and a great increase of children . . . temporal prosperity will be promoted by a remarkable blessing from heaven.

—*Works*, III

Knowledge

Knowledge is the key that first opens the hard heart, enlarges the affections, and opens the way for men into the kingdom of heaven.

—*Works*, V

Religion: Its Nature and Function

True religion, in great part, consists in holy affections . . . the more vigorous and sensible exercises of the inclination and will of the soul.

—*Religious Affections*, 1746

Virtue

True virtue . . . is that consent, propensity, and union of heart to being in general, which is immediately exercised in a general good-will.

—*The Nature of True Virtue*, 1758

World and God

The end of God's creating the world, was to prepare a kingdom for his Son . . . which should remain to all eternity.

—*History of the Work of Redemption, Works, IV*, 1754

8. Celebrate anniversaries with other Christians.

The following anniversaries in 1983 are especially suitable for observing with other denominations.

250th: The Founding of Georgia and the Beginning of the Salzeberger's Migration to Georgia (1733).

225th: The Influence of James Hutton, a Moravian, in the Conversion of John Wesley (1758).

225th: John Woolman's Speech, Awakening Social Concern (1758).

200th: Publication of Johann Gottfried Eichhorn's "Introduction To The Old Testament" (1783).

200th: Founding of the Protestant Episcopal Church in America (1783).

175th: The Death of David Zeigenberger, Moravian Missionary to the Indians (1808).

150th: The Abolition of Slavery in England and the Death of William Wilberforce (1833).

150th: William Keble's Speech, Launching the Oxford Movement (1833).

150th: Robert Grant's Hymn, "O Worship The King" (1833).

150th: John Henry Newman's Hymn, "Lead Kindly Light" (1833).

150th: James Montgomery's Hymn, "Lord, Pour Thy Spirit" (1833).

150th: Henry Oliver's Hymn Tune, *Federal Street*, and Alexi Lwoff's Russian Hymn (1833).

125th: St. Bernadette's Vision at Lourdes (1858).

125th: Catherine Winkworth's Hymn Translations (1858).

125th: William How's Hymn, "We Give Thee But Thine Own" (1858).

125th: Edward Caswall's Hymn Translation, "When Morning Gilds the Skies" (1858).

125th: George Duffield's Hymn, "Stand Up, Stand Up For Jesus" (1858).

100th: Timothy Matthew's Hymn Tune, *Saxby*, and Arthur Mann's *Angel's Story* (1883).

75th: The Social Creed of the Federal Council of Churches (1908).

75th: The Death of Hymn Writer, Walter C. Smith ("Immortal, Invisible") (1908).

75th: The Death of Composer, Lewis Redner (*St. Louis:* "O Little Town of Bethlehem") (1908).

75th: The Death of Composer, Edward Husband (*St. Edith:* "O Jesus, Thou Art Standing") (1908).

50th: The Death of Hymn Writer, Henry Van Dyke ("Joyful, Joyful, We Adore Thee", "Jesus, Thou Divine Companion") (1933).

25th: Pope John XXIII's Election (1958).

25th: The Publication of J. B. Philip's "New Testament in Modern English" (1958).

9. Prepare to celebrate anniversaries in 1984 and beyond.

The following anniversaries are coming up in 1984.

500th: Birthday of Ulrich Zwingli (1484).

475th: Birthday of John Calvin (1509).

425th: Philip Melanchthon's Formal Admission Into The Reformed Church (1559).

400th: The Death of William of Nassau, Prince of Orange (1584).

300th: The Revoking of Massachusett's Charter (1684).

275th: The Flight from the Palatinate and the Beginnings of the German Reformed Migration to America (1709).

275th: John Frederick Hager's Arrival in New York and His Ordination (1709).

275th: Solomon Stoddard's "An Appeal To The Learned" (1709).

200th: "Brief Observations on the Doctrine of Universal Salvation", by Jonathan Edwards, the younger (1784).

200th: The Christmas Conference in Baltimore that Provoked James O'Kelley's Departure from the Methodist Church (1784).

200th: William Stoy's Election at the Pennsylvania Legislature (1784).

150th: The Death of Friedrich Ernst Daniel Schleiermacher (1834).

150th: Publication of "Psalms and Hymns For the Use of the Reformed Church in the United States of America" (1834).

125th: Franklin Woodbury Fisk's Joining the Faculty of Chicago Theological Seminary (1859).

125th: The Founding of a Mission House by the Classis of Sheboygan (1859).

125th: The Founding of the German United Evangelical Synod of Northwest (1859).

125th: The Publication of "Cantata Domino: A Collection of Chants, Hymns, and Tunes", edited by Lewis H. Steiner and Henry Schwing (1859).

125th: The Publication of *Deutsches Gesangbuch*, edited by Dr. Philip Schaff (1859).

100th: The First Reformed Church Organized in Japan (1884).

100th: Publication of "Tunes of Worship", edited by Henry Schwing (1884).

75th: Hymns by Ozora Stearns Davis (1909).

75th: Publication of the Evangelical Synod's "Gesangbuch der Evangelischen Kirche" (1909).

75th: The Death of Daniel Marsh, Hymnwriter (1909).

50th: The Death of David Bruning, Composer (1934).

50th: The Founding of the Evangelical and Reformed Church (1934).

25th: The Statement of Faith of the United Church of Christ (1959).

The following may be celebrated with other Christians in 1984:

775th: The Conversion of St. Francis of Assisi (1209).

600th: The Death of John Wyclif (1384).

225th: The Death of George Frederick Handel (1759).

125th: William Bradbury's Tunes (1859).

25th: The Death of Bishop Eivind Josef Berggrav, Ecumenist (1959).

BIBLIOGRAPHY

A History of the Christian Church, Williston Walker. Charles Scribner's Sons, New York, 1944.

A History of the Christian Church In the South, Durward T. Stokes and William T. Scott. Elon College, North Carolina, 1973.

A History of the Congregationalist Churches in the United States, American History Series, Williston Walker. Charles Scribner's Sons, New York, 1894.

A History of the Evangelical and Reformed Church, David Dunn, Paul N. Crusius, Josais Friedli, Theophil W. Menzel, Carl E. Schneider, William Toth, and James Wagner. The Christian Education Press, Philadelphia, 1961.

American Christianity: An Historical Interpretation With Representative Documents, Volume I, 1607–1820, H. Shelton Smith, Robert T. Handy, and Lefferts A. Loetscher. Charles Scribner's Sons, New York, 1960.

American Christianity: An Historical Interpretation With Representative Documents, Volume II, 1820–1960, H. Shelton Smith, Robert T. Handy, and Lefferts A. Loetscher. Charles Scribner's Sons, New York, 1963.

American Faith, Ernest Sutherland Bates. W. W. Norton & Company, Inc. Publishers, New York, 1940.

A Religious History of America, Edwin Scott Gaustad. Harper & Row, Publishers, New York, 1966.

A Religious History of the American People, Sydney E. Ahlstrom. Yale University Press, New Haven and London, 1972.

Churches and Sects of Christendom, Juergen Ludwig Neve. Lutheran Publishing House, Blair, Neb., Revised Edition (1948, c. 1944).

Bibliography

Congregationalists in America, Albert E. Dunning. J.A. Hill & Co., Publishers, New York, 1894.

Guide To The Pilgrim Hymnal, Albert C. Ronander and Ethel K. Porter. United Church Press, Philadelphia and Boston, 1966.

Handbook To The Hymnal, William Chalmers Covert and Calvin Weiss Lauffer. Presbyterian Board of the Christian Education, Philadelphia, 1936.

Historic Manual of the Reformed Church in the United States, Joseph Henry Dubbs. Lancaster, 1885.

History and Program of the United Church of Christ. United Church Press, 1978.

History of American Congregationalism, Gaius Glenn Atkins and Frederick L. Fagley. The Pilgrim Press, Boston and Chicago, 1942.

History of the Classis of Lancaster of the Eastern Synod of the Reformed Church in the United States, edited by Daniel G. Glass, C. George Bachman, Harry E. Shepardson, John F. Franz, and J. N. Levan. The Classis of Lancaster, New Holland, Pa., 1942.

History of Religion in the United States, Clifton E. Olmstead. Prentice-Hall, Englewood Cliffs, N.J., 1960.

Jonathan Edwards: The Narrative, James A. Stewart. Kregel Publications, Grand Rapids, Michigan, 1957.

Lives of Christian Ministers, P. J. Kernodle. The Central Publishing Company, Richmond, Va., 1909.

Luther, Robert H. Fischer. Lutheran Church Press, 1966.

Lyric Religion: The Romance of Immortal Hymns, H. Augustine Smith. D. Appleton-Century Company, New York and London, 1931.

Masterpieces of Christian Literature: In Summary Form, Ed. Frank N. Magill. Harper and Row, Publishers; New York, Evanston and London, 1963.

No Ivory Tower: The Story of the Chicago Theological Seminary, Arthur Cushman McGiffert, Jr. The Chicago Theological Seminary, 1965.

On The Trail of the U.C.C.: A Historical Atlas of the United Church of Christ, ed. Carolyn E. Goddard. United Church Press, New York.

Religion in Colonial America, William Warren Sweet. Scribner, New York, 1943.

The Age of Reason Begins, The Story of Civilization, Part VII, Will and Ariel Durant. Simon and Schuster, New York, 1961.

The Christian Denomination and Christian Doctrine, Simon Addison Bennett. The Christian Publishing Association, Dayton, Ohio.

The Congregational Way, Marion L. Starkey; Religion in America Series, ed. Charles W. Ferguson. Doubleday & Company, Inc. Garden City, New York, 1966.

172

Bibliography

The German Church on the American Frontier, Carl E. Schneider. Eden Publishing House, St. Louis, Missouri, 1939.

The Gospel In Hymns, Albert Edward Bailey. Charles Scribner's Sons, New York, 1950.

The Historical Handbook of the Reformed Church, James Isaac Good. The Heidelberg Press, Philadelphia, 1915.

The Hymnal 1940 Companion, The Joint Commission On the Revision of the Hymnal of the Protestant Episcopal Church in the United States of America. The Church Pension Fund, New York, 1951.

The Reformation, The Story of Civilization, Part VI, Will Durant. Simon and Schuster, New York, 1957.

The Story of Our Hymns: The Handbook to the Hymnal of the Evangelical and Reformed Church, Armin Haeussler. Eden Publishing House, St. Louis, Missouri, 1952.

Words of Faith, Loring D. Chase, Confirmation Education Series. United Church Press, Boston and Philadelphia, 1968.